Affiliate Marketing
The Online Marketing Blueprint for Internet Marketing

By: Keith Fugate

Free Bonus: Join Our Book Club and Receive Free Gifts Instantly

Click Below For Your Bonus:
https://success321.leadpages.co/freebodymindsoul/

author or copyright owner. Legal action will be pursued if this is breached.

Disclaimer Notice:

Please note the information contained within this document is for educational and entertainment purposes only. Every attempt has been made to provide accurate, up to date and reliable complete information. No warranties of any kind are expressed or implied. Readers acknowledge that the author is not engaging in the rendering of legal, financial, medical or professional advice.

By reading this document, the reader agrees that under no circumstances are we responsible for any losses, direct or indirect, which are incurred as a result of the use of information contained within this document, including, but not limited to, — errors, omissions, or inaccuracies.

TABLE OF CONTENTS

Introduction

The 90s saw the rise of multiple phenomena – Jim Carrey, for one, and bands such as Nirvana and Pearl Jam heralding a new genre of music for another. But no phenomenon was as life-changing and even as world-changing as the world wide web. The web that reached into every home, office, network, and continent, this was perhaps the first truly global phenomenon. In the two decades since, nothing has changed. The World Wide Web or internet is still as big a thing as it ever was, if not bigger.

Naturally, it did not take long for companies to realize what a truly marvelous marketing platform they had with the internet. Here was a new opportunity to expand their customer base into areas they hadn't even dreamed of before. When search engines came to the fore, they changed the way the world searched for information, products and services. Commerce became e-commerce and marketing became linked to terms such as CPM and, eventually, affiliate marketing.

In this book, we will trace the history of affiliate marketing, explain exactly what it is and how it works, and determine the advantages and disadvantages. At the end of this book, you will know how to benefit from affiliate marketing whether you are the affiliate or the merchant.

I hope that by the time you've read this book, you will have a thorough understanding of what affiliate marketing is. I also hope that you will gain a good perspective of this type of marketing to determine whether or not it can be utilized by you. Finally, I hope this book answers whatever questions you have with regards to this field.

Thank you for buying this book. I hope you have a pleasant time reading it.

Chapter 1: What is Affiliate Marketing?

If you have done research on marketing on the internet, the chances are that you have come across the term 'affiliate marketing' at least once. You may not have explored the term or understood what it is, but you must at least have heard a mention of it. If not, don't worry. The following paragraphs and chapters will help you gain a good understanding of this term.

Affiliate marketing is a type of performance-based advertising that pays for performance in advertising. In this type of advertising or marketing, the purchaser pays the advertiser only when the results of the advertising are measurable. This type of advertising is becoming more prominent with the spread of the internet since tools such as Google Analytics and many other apps make it possible for a company to know the user response to its advertisements.

In affiliate marketing, the company hires one or more affiliates. These affiliates do the marketing for the company on the net. Based on the number of visitors or customers they bring in through their marketing efforts, the affiliates are paid by the company. Put simply; you can make money online when you are rewarded by a business for promoting their service, product or website. From the perspective of a company, you can hire someone else to market whatever it is that you are selling and pay them based on the results, i.e. the number of customers they are able to attract through their marketing.

Affiliate marketing works through four players – the merchant who is also known as the brand or the retailer, the network that contains the offers an affiliate can select from and that also takes care of the payments to the affiliate, the affiliates themselves who are also known as the publishers and, of course, the customers. As it has expanded, affiliate marketing has become more and more complex with another tier of players, such as super-affiliates and affiliate management agencies, coming in.

Many people often confuse affiliate marketing with referral marketing. It is a common enough mistake to make, especially when you consider that both types of marketing use third parties to attract visitors and customers for the retailers. However, the key difference between the two is that; in affiliate

12

marketing sales are driven purely by financial motivations. In referral marketing, on the other hand, personal relationships and the trust therein are used to drive sales.

At the moment, compared to other marketing strategies, affiliate marketing still holds a relatively low profile. Advertisers frequently overlook this marketing strategy, their attention captured by other strategies such as search engine optimization and website syndication. However, many e-retailers still consider affiliate marketing a major part of their marketing strategies.

Chapter 2: History of Affiliate Marketing

Origin

Revenue sharing or paying commissions for a business that has been referred is not a new concept. In fact, this concept came into being way before the advent of the internet and affiliate marketing. The transition of revenue share principles to the mainstream e-commerce began in November 1994, approximately four years after the implementation of the world wide web.

The concept of affiliate marketing on the internet was conceived by, implemented and patented by a man named William J. Tobin, the man who created PC Flowers and Gifts. PC Flowers and Gifts was launched in 1989 on the Prodigy Network and operated in that service for seven years until 1996. By 1993, PC Flowers & Gifts had generated a sales amount that exceeded $6 million per year on the service of Prodigy Network. In 1998, PC Flowers and Gifts created a business model of paying a commission on sales to the Prodigy Network.

In conjunction with IBM, because it owned half of Prodigy, Tobin ventured on to the internet with a PC Flowers and Gifts beta version in 1994. Within a year, a commercial version of the PC Flowers and Gifts website had been launched. The company also had 2600 affiliate marketing partners on the internet. Realizing the value of the business model he had started, Tobin sent in an application for patents on tracking and affiliate marketing on January 22, 1996, and was issued U.S. Patent number 6,141,666 on Oct 31, 2000. Tobin took it even further to receive a Japanese Patent (number 4021941) in 2007 and U.S. Patent 7,505,913 in 2009 for his part in affiliate marketing and tracking. In 1998, PC Flowers and Gifts carried out a merger with Fingerhut along with Federated Department Stores.

One of the first innovators in the field of affiliate marketing was cyber erotica, which had a cost per click program.

The innovation continued with CDNOW which started the BuyWeb program in November 1994. The idea came to CDNOW that websites that had to do with music could list or review albums that they felt that the visitors to the website might be interested in buying. What the websites could do was offer a link that would take prospective buyers to the CDNOW web site where they could make their purchases. This whole idea first came into being thanks to conversations with Geffen Records, a music label. What Geffen wanted was to be able to sell their artists' music directly on their website. However, they did not want to have to create this feature themselves. Instead, they talked to CDNOW about a program which would let CDNOW take care of the orders. They discovered that CDNOW had the capability to link from the artist on its own website to Geffen's official website. This would bypass the homepage for CDNOW and go straight to the music page of the artist.

In July 1996, Amazon, via Amazon.com, started an associate program which allowed the associates to place text links or banners for individual books on their site. The program also allowed them to link directly to the Amazon home page. When people who visited the associate's site clicked through to Amazon and bought a book, Amazon gave a commission to the associate. Amazon was by no means the first company to offer such incentive in the form of the affiliate program. However, its program was the first to really catch on and eventually served as a business model for other such programs.

February 2000 saw Amazon making the announcement that a patent had been granted to the company on certain parts of an affiliate program. The application had been submitted in June 1997. This was before most affiliate programs came into being but not before certain programs such as PC Flowers & Gifts.com which submitted its application in October 1994, AutoWeb.com which did the same in October 1995, BrainPlay.com/Kbkids.com in January 1996, EPage in April 1996 and quite a few others.

Historic Development

Affiliate marketing has grown quickly since its inception. At the beginning of the internet era, e-commerce web sites were looked at more as a fun marketing toy, but soon played a prominent role in businesses overall marketing plans, and for some business savvy professionals, it grew to a bigger business than the existing offline business. One report indicated that affiliate networks generated a total sales amount of £2.16 billion in the United Kingdom in 2006. In 2005, the sales estimates had hovered around the £1.35 billion mark. The research team at MarketingSherpa came up with the estimate that around the world, in 2006, the earnings of affiliates came to around US$6.5 billion in commissions and bounty. The sources ranged from retail to gambling to telecom to education to travel and also methods of lead generation apart from the contextual advertising programs.

Affiliate marketing was most popular in sectors such as gambling, file sharing services, retail industries and adult entertainment in 2006. The three divisions that were expected to experience the highest level of growth were the cellular phone, financial, and the travel sectors. Following behind these sectors were the entertainment/gaming sector and service sectors that were internet-related (ISPs). At this time, several of the affiliate solution providers anticipated receivingan increased interest from marketers related to business and advertisers wanting to use affiliate marketing as a part of their marketing mix.

Web 2.0

Websites and/or services that were based on Web 2.0 concepts, such as blogging and interactive communities, have had a huge impact on the affiliate marketing world as well. These platforms allowed improved communication between merchants and affiliates. Affiliate marketing channels have also been opened to writers, independent website owners, and bloggers, thanks to

Web 2.0 platforms. Publishers who don't have very high levels of web traffic use contextual ads to place affiliate ads on websites.

The way ads are presented to visitors by brands, ad networks, and companies has also changed because of the advent of new types of media. Let's take YouTube for example. Video makers on YouTube are permitted to embed ads through the affiliate network that Google has. Unscrupulous affiliates have begun to find it more difficult to make money thanks to new advancements. These advancements can detect fraudulent affiliates who are just starting out and identify them to the affiliate marketing community faster and more efficiently.

Chapter 3: How to Start an Affiliate Marketing Business

You can earn commissions through affiliate marketing by selling services or products that are on offer from other companies. Affiliate marketing has become an efficient way to earn more money while sitting at home. In addition, becoming an affiliate for well-known companies is quite easy. Here's how you can do it.

1. Sell What You Know

When you're starting out it is best to stick to marketing services and products that you know and understand. This is known as "picking your niche" in the online marketing community. Look for a niche that is either about what you do or about what you're interested in – in other words, look for something related either to your job or to your hobbies and interests.

For instance, if you're a blogger you're better off selling books than fishing gear (unless, of course, you blog about fishing). Your marketing efforts are more likely to bear fruit if you focus on selling what you're familiar with.

2. Start a Website Relevant to Your Niche

When you decide to start out as an affiliate, the first thing that the companies you approach will want to know is what website you intend to sell their stuff on. This is because the companies need to make sure that their image and reputation isn't damaged by what the website publishes.

Starting a website is no longer a job just for the professionals. Plenty of sites such as WordPress can help you set up your own website. Ensure that there is content on your website that isn't sales-oriented. The whole point here is that your site should leave the impression that you know what you're talking about.

3. Research Affiliate Programs

Don't just go for the first affiliate program that you find. Look for one that is related to your niche and offers those types of services and products.

One program you can try is Amazon. Since it's a marketplace, just about anything is available there, which makes it more likely that products from your niche will be available there. The program is a popular one and a great place to begin your foray into affiliate marketing.

Another option you can consider is Clickbank. It is quite popular among affiliate marketers. The reason is simple – companies on Clickbank have the reputation of offering very good commissions.

4. Join an Affiliate Program

Joining an affiliate program is almost always free of charge. You should probably be wary if a program wants your credit card information just to make you an affiliate. The chances are that it is a scam. The reputable companies don't charge anything for allowing you to become an affiliate with their affiliate programs.

Companies will ask you for your PayPal or bank account information. Don't be alarmed. This is simple so that they can pay your commissions, not so that they can take your money.

5. Add Affiliate Links in Your Content

A great way to earn a commission without earning a reputation for just being a "sales" site is to incorporate the affiliate links into your content. This makes people more inclined to click on the links and, of course, if they buy something you get a commission.

For example, say you're writing a review about a book you recently read and liked. Make the name of the book a link to Amazon's site that shows your visitors the prices for the hardcover, soft cover and kindle versions of that book. Your readers can then determine what suits them most and buy it.

The good news here is that it is very easy to get links to the sites of these companies. How you get the links will differ, of course, but finding the links to the products you want to sell isn't difficult at all.

6. In Your Sidebar, Be Sure to Include Visual Ads

Most websites have a sidebar; yours probably does too. The sidebar can be a great spot to place visual ads for the products that your site discusses.

Again, you'll see that companies that have affiliate programs make it simple for you to get the links and images that will make your visitors go to their sites. Most of the time, all you have to do is copy and paste code into the sidebar.

7. Continue Producing Content Relevant to Your Niche

If you want to continue earning commissions, you'll need to ensure that people keep visiting your site. In order to do this, you'll need to ensure that you keep updating your site frequently and regularly with relevant content. Digital marketers call this "content marketing."

Just any old content won't do. Your content has to be good if you want them to keep coming back and, more importantly, click on the affiliate links that you have and buy stuff.

8. Use Analytics to Measure Your Success

Consider analytics a tool that gives you information about what you've sold, how it was sold and to whom you sold it. Luckily for you, there is analytics on most affiliate marketing sites that can prove to be quite helpful. They will analyze all the information from your site and tell you what is working out for you and what isn't.

If you want to know and understand the demographics of your visitors, Google Analytics is your best bet. Once you have an idea of the demographic, you can create content for it.

You also need to keep an eye out for posts that have the highest number of visitors. You can think about adding affiliate marketing links to posts that are getting more visitors.

If you're really serious about affiliate marketing, then you need to find out what works and concentrate on that. Remove what doesn't work. You can find out what types of ads are working for you and what aren't through the analytics that the company provides. Obviously, you'll want to use the ones that are working and remove the ones that aren't.

9. Prepare for Taxes

If commissions are pouring in through affiliate marketing (or even if they're coming in at a slow but steady rate), you will need to pay taxes. After all, it is income. The companies that you've partnered with will send you a 1099 form at the beginning of the year. However, don't wait for them to do that. Report your income to the IRS when you're supposed to.

If you are a sole proprietor or LLC and that's how you're running the affiliate marketing, you'll need to report the 1099 income on Schedule C – Profit or Loss from Business.

If on the other hand, your business is being run like a C or S corporation, the income needs to be reported on Schedule K1.

10. Expand Your Business

Your business is going to go one of two ways – either it'll expand or it'll contract. This is why growth is necessary. If your business shrinks the returns, you will get keep reducing.

Don't just stick to marketing one product. Keep looking for new stuff that you can sell. Keep going through the different affiliate site. Also, keep an eye out for new businesses that have just started affiliate marketing programs. If they have something that you think will work out well for you, approach them with a partnership.

Another thing to keep doing is promoting your business online regularly and frequently. You can use email, social media and various other ways to market your business so that your visitors keep returning because they know that you provide good deals on services and products that you market (well, actually, it's the company that provides them, but you get what I mean).

11. Delegate Tedious Tasks To Others

Once your affiliate marketing starts to turn a profit, you'll need to focus on growth. This means that you'll also need to delegate the regular stuff to someone else. Of course, this means hiring labor and that means more expense, but in the end, it is worth it. The delegation will give you the time you need to come up with different ways to promote your business and help it grow as much as possible.

12. Automate What You Can

Digital marketing tools can really help you decrease your own workload so that you can concentrate on other aspects of your business. Most of these tools are paid, but the investment is worth it.

The whole point here is for you to be able to concentrate on growing your business while your employees and tools handle the routine stuff.

Before delving into the affiliate networks, let's look at some of the ways to evaluate the product or service you choose.

5 Means to Evaluate a Product or Service

As an affiliate, this is the most significant aspect of the process. There's no point in scrutinizing affiliate program details until you find a product that you know your visitors will buy.

1. Is the product or service relevant to your site or page?

Financial service banners on a beauty site look out of place. If you are working as an affiliate, this kind of intermingling serve only to distract the visitor's focus.

2. Is the company's site eye-catching and functional?

The company's site should be enticing and highly professional. The sites that have broken links and are difficult to navigate are not so promising. Don't direct your visitors to low-quality sites as they may damage your reputation.

3. Does the program offer great products/services at sensible prices?

As a seller, you must believe in the products/services you sell. If you are not knowledgeable about the product how can you market it effectively? In addition, also check the pricing of the products as they should be reasonable.

4. Purchase and test the products you are going to promote.

You should purchase a majority of the products you are promoting. Having first-hand experience with an item gives you the advantage over other affiliates that are selling the exact same product. If the commission is going to be 25%, you will only need to make as few as four sales to earn your money back.

5. Does the company provide excellent customer service?

This is important, although not directly pertaining to you. You may receive emails from the affiliate program customers because the company is not replying to their queries. Unfortunately, there is really nothing that you can do about this.

You can offer to pass their request along using the email and contact information that was given to you but keep in mind that if the desired result is not met, it will reflect on you and your business.

Chapter 4: A detailed account on Affiliate Networks

Once you have selected your niche, you have to find the merchants who sell similar products and services. Finding the merchant can be a troublesome task, so that's where the affiliate networks come into play. The affiliate networks can help you connect with copious merchants who sell products/services relevant to your niche. With the increasing advancement and competition in the advertising industry, web merchants are looking upon affiliate networks to supply them the best affiliates- who can excel their business through unique and creative promotion strategies.

Affiliate networks act as a third party and functions as a middleman between the affiliates and merchants. Broadly speaking, it is a central unit where merchants can enlist their products and services with the appropriate guidelines for the affiliates, and the affiliates can pursue different programs according to their likings. The affiliate network company keeps track of the sales statistics, makes sure the marketing tools are available and scrutinizes the process of commission checks to affiliates.

For merchants, joining an affiliate network places a great many avid affiliates ideal for the job on their doorsteps. Because of the benefits affiliates bring in the shape of qualified traffic, the merchants are glad to pay them and the affiliate networks as well. For affiliates, the services of affiliate networks are equally valuable. You don't have to pay any upfront fee as joining is free, and the hectic task of finding and selecting the merchant is simplified with the aid of categorical search facilities. Those who are familiar with the nitty-gritty of the affiliate marketing seek the assistance of the affiliate networks as they tend to offer high-quality programs in general.

Most of the affiliate networks ask for preliminary requirements like payment method and contact details just once in the beginning. After being selected into the network, you can apply to different merchant programs. In some cases, the merchant considers and responds to your request immediately while in some settings, it may take up to a week. Upon approval from the merchant, the marketing material is readily available for you to work with. The HTML codes for banners and text links are usually generated with a mere click of the mouse. You are just required to cut and paste the code into your website pages. The banners mostly consume a lot of bandwidths, so they are usually hosted by the affiliate network. The affiliate network companies don't bombard you with unnecessary emails. Instead, you will receive notifications regarding the new merchants associated with the network, and stuff relevant to your site. It can save you time when sorting through your mailbox.

Some networks also give an indication of the merchants who are running low on funds, so you can cease their promotion activity for the time being; just to make sure that your time isn't wasted. Mostly networks compile a single monthly paycheck of all the merchants you cater. But this trend differs from network to network. The most promising aspect of joining an affiliate network is the ease that you don't have to visit the merchants' site again separately to calculate your revenue. This can save you enormous amount of time.

Each affiliate network operates in a different fashion. I would like to mention some of the best affiliate networks in the market. I suggest you visit each and every one of them, so you can make a proper choice.

34

ClickBank

ClickBank is in business for seventeen years. They have over 6 million unique products to offer. They have an enormous customer base reaching over 200 million across the globe. They primarily offer CPS and real-time tracking for affiliate programs. Their one-page application procedure is the shortest you will see. The company enlists merchants' products on the basis of their popularity and demand. There is no waiting for the approval from different merchants. It is simple and straightforward, you are just required to find the merchant of your likings, and start getting paid upon approval. Creating links is quite easy, simply click on the commission percentage link; located opposite to the products' title. After clicking you will be directed to a window to enter your Clickbank's ID and the link is automatically generated after you provide the information. Their links are exceptionally short and therefore easy to promote within email campaigns. Clickbank withholds back some portion of the checks for security purpose, and the holdbacks are credited back to the account after the probation period.

clixGalore

clixGlore has over tens of thousands of affiliates and merchants across its three networks in the USA, Australia, and the UK. They follow CPA, CPC, CPS programs integrated with a multi-tier system, and most importantly the payments are monthly checks.

clixGalore has a user-friendly interface. When doing a search by category for merchants, the results pop up like the search engine format with highlighted merchant banners at the top of each page. It's evident that these merchants have paid for advertising, most probably within the network. The listings below those highlighted are some pointers of descriptions of the program and product, with the commission rates and a link to join the setting. The only search function that produced good comparative results was from a tab on the homepage by the name of 'Search Top Performing Programs.' That returned a table with columns listing product titles, commission rates, numbers of banners, and approved, pending and declined application requests. Each row includes a join link.

CJ Affiliate

CJ (Customer Junction) affiliate is the subsidiary of the Conversant; online advertising company. CJ affiliate follows CPA, CPC, CPS programs, and the payments are consolidated into one monthly paycheck. Don't get confused when you first enter CJ as they usually refer the affiliates as publishers. Their application procedure is also simple, and there are no restrictions in the sign up process. However, those sites containing obscene, abusive, defamatory, violent, bigoted, hate-ridden, and illegal content are restricted. Turnaround time on the application is very rapid. Here are some of the reasons to choose CJ affiliate as your ideal affiliate network.

The site's interface is instinctive and user-friendly: Unlike some other affiliate network interfaces, the designers at Customer junction have done a fantastic job in creating the interface that is easy to navigate and use.

Finding program is simple and quick: You are just required to do a simple search for an advertiser, link, or product, by entering a keyword into a search box. All relevant data is then returned. However, some networks allow merchants to place themselves in irrelevant groups which makes finding appropriate advertisers much trickier.

Statistics regarding merchant performance are available: Statistics depicting how well each merchant converts site visitors into sales (conversion rate) can be seen. You can also see the average commissions paid to affiliates for every 100 clicks for the previous week. The company utilizes a 'dollar sign' rating system, and you can see the volume of commissions paid by a particular advertiser, relative to the rest of the merchants.

The dollar sign rankings are deciphered as:

• $$$$$=95th percentile and above

• $$$$=80-94th percentile

• $$$=60-79th percentile

• $$=40-59th percentile

• $=39th percentile and below

• Blank=No commissions earned

Commission rates are easily accessible and are not hard to find: At most of the affiliate networks, if you are looking to find the commission rates of a particular merchant, you may get a headache searching them. However, at CJ, commission percentage or dollar value per sale/lead, are prominently revealed alongside each advertiser's entry.

The information available is vast: Clicking on the advertiser's name takes you to a page giving a written description of the company, their product, and the affiliate program. Below the description, you can also explore more about the merchant as abundant information is available, and finally, the contact link can be used if you find the work appealing.

The merchants and company won't spam you with infinite offers daily: You can choose not to receive an email from merchants whose programs you have joined. That email is then delivered to your mailbox in CJ's system.

Getting in touch with merchants is super easy: Within the company's mail system all the programs you are currently affiliated with are enlisted separated.

Simply select the one you want to contact, write your message in the accompanying box and send it.

Getting linking codes and graphics is simple: Simply hit the 'get links' tab, choose from the wide collection of text and graphic links returned, and then copy and paste the code that pops up on your screen. The images will not get saved to your PC. All the graphics are stored on Commission Junction's servers. That's how you save your bandwidth. You can also create your own 'SmartZones,' which are assortments of rotating links that may contain links from the same, or many different advertisers. Each link within the SmartZone is assigned a weight that determines how often it will display in relation to the other links within the SmartZone. You get one small piece of javascript to place on your page, and then when you want to add or remove banners, you do so through the CJ interface.

Tremendous capability for examining your statistics: You can view more than 100 customizable reports with real-time data through the CJ Account Manager. Affiliates can generate reports on their individual links, transactions, and their individual merchants.

Brilliant help supports system: The help system can be searched by directory, glossary, contents, or a simple search. If you still can't find the answer you are looking for, simply seek the help of company's representative through an email. They always respond within the same day.

40

Commissions are consolidated into one paycheck: You can fill out your deposit slips at a much rapid rate. If you are not comfortable with deposit slips, direct deposit is an available option. If you join no other affiliate networks, be sure to join Commission Junction. Their client list is impressive. A few of Commission Junction's clients include Boden, Costume Express, Discount Mags, H&R Block, Home Depot, HSN, InterContinental Hotels Group, RingCentral, Tire Rack, and TurboTax; etc.

Commission Soup

Commission soup primarily follows CPA and CPS programs with real-time tracking and multi-tier (you can hire your own affiliate to help with the advertising) facility. They specialize in offering financial-niche related products. Commission Soup follow strict guidelines when it comes to email marketing. Make sure that you follow those guidelines. Their supporting staff is collaborative, and upon request, their representative will soon get back to you. Signup restrictions are trifling, including the rights not to accept sites that are international marketing sites, poorly designed, poor quality sites, adult sites that promote pornography or sexual material, and are harmful in the whole context.

Most of the affiliate networks don't allow affiliates outside the US or the sites that are operational outside US. It's always surprising why it matters where a site is based if it can direct US citizens to their site. Luckily there are some networks where sanity prevails; companies like commission soup acknowledge the importance of Internet marketing as a worldwide activity. They don't discriminate against non-resident US citizens as they welcome skillful affiliate marketers around the globe; as long as their site is targeting the US audience. Some of their current clients include Primor, AccountNow, Applied Bank, Credit One Bank, FlexShopper, and RewardsRunner, etc.

Dark Blue Affiliate Network

This affiliate network follows CPA and CPS program with real-time tracking facility, however, they don't allow the multi-tier program. Dark Blue's application process is an easy step-by-step directed process. You are first asked for your email address, and by the time you've have entered your particulars, your Dark Blue program key will be waiting for you in your email. Simply enter the key and start earning money by promoting their merchants' products and services. The approval process may be automatic, but the company still has its standards. Your website must not contain or link to material or content that is adult in nature, obscene, hateful, offensive, or is libelous, defatory, or appears to invade a person's privacy or rights or is otherwise illegal. They've also specified that you must not place any statements on or near the Dark Blue advertising banners requesting or insisting the surfers to visit your website.

Dark Blue has a very striking and relatively easy to use interface. However, their system for locating advertisers is not alluring. The category navigation that first pops up after clicking the specific tab appears to be ordered according to market demand. In general, travel, health, and fitness products are the most searched products on the Internet. The best way to find the category is through an alphabetical arrangement; most preferably if you are not sure what to choose.

LeadHound

LeadHound was launched in December 1999. They also deal in the affiliate software. The company follows CPC, CPS, and CPA program. They also provide the facilities of real-time tracking and multi-tier program. The sign-up process is split into three different sections, but it won't be troublesome for you. In Campaigns page list the presence of average revenue per click opposite each product and service is probably the most promising feature of LeadHound. This kind of information helps you in estimating the amount you are going to spend on the pay per click advertising campaign for a specific product. The ease of checking statistics at LeadHound is also appreciable as they monitor it in real-time. The display is amazing and easy to use, and all the functions are self-explanatory.

Rakuten Linkshare

Rakuten claims to be the most successful pay per performance affiliate network in the world. They have over 90,000 products with a customer base of over 18 million worldwide. The company offers CPA, CPC, and CPS programs, and they have also integrated real-time tracking and multi-tier marketing facility in their system. Like all other affiliate networks, their interface is easy to use. In fact, the create link tab enables you to see the list of all of your present merchants. This is something better when comparing it with CJ affiliates where the merchant's list is not just a click away. Furthermore, if you are looking to find the detailed information (contact and commission rates) of the merchant and their program rapidly; Linkshare can provide you with the facility. You can also view whether any of your joined programs have been put on hold or discontinued.

The affiliate links at Linkshare are longer relative to the CJ's affiliate links which are short. Short links are far better for use in email campaigns. If a link is too long, it breaks, and the page doesn't open at your subscriber's end when they click on the link. However, this issue can be overcome by the use of link redirects. For this purpose, you could use the Affiliate Link Cloaker software and get shorter links. The software is also helpful in providing safety from commission theft.

Linkshare has established their premium partner program for excellent merchants. The eligibility criteria are fulfilled by the ideal merchant program that:

- Utilizes company's check-cutting service.

- Recompenses affiliates on a monthly basis.

- Punctually and rapidly sanctions affiliate payments, so affiliates are paid at a faster rate.

- Allows seven or more return days (not valid for merchants who are associated with pay per click programs).

- Has delivered valid and comprehensive contact information in their profile.

- Is active and in good standing.

Their statistics reporting technique is remarkable, and you can create many different types of reports. Their clients include: 7 for all mankind, Clarins, Lancome Paris, passerelle, Macy's, mango, monsoon accessorize, music notes, Sephora, sports craft, vans, viator, Vince Camuto, vision direct, Walmart, Wayfair, wine, Zimmermann

Quinstreet

The company has 17 years of experience in performance marketing. They follow CPA and CPS programs, their time tracking is a bit delayed, but they provide multi-tier marketing facility. Their site's design is phenomenal. The signup procedure is simple, and they do not even ask for your address details. Nonetheless, you can provide them with details later once you are eligible to receive the check for one of the merchants. The data about each merchant's commission rates and schedule can be seen effortlessly. You just have to click on the merchant's profile to get the entire relevant information. Presently, their chief client verticals are the financial and education services industries. They also have an existence in the home services, business to business (B2B), and medical and heath industries.

ShareaSale

The company follows CPA, CPS, and CPC programs. Real-time tracking and multi-tier program facilities are available, but an additional fee and charges are placed on each new affiliate. There is no substantial restriction in the application process; however, you must have a valid email address and a valid website. They also recommend that affiliates should have a top notch domain name. They have an incredible criterion to cut out spammers from their system. Once your application is approved and you enter the interface, you will be informed that you are running on limited membership, and you will not be able to apply to pay per sale or pay per lead program until you generate at least some worth of valid CPA transactions. This is how they cut out the pool of spammers.

As far as their interface is concerned, it is a bit tough to look at for longer periods of time. Yellow links on white backgrounds are responsible for giving you eyestrains. It is very difficult to concentrate if you are to work for longer periods.

The simple search for merchants is a little slow and unwieldy. Clicking on a category returns some merchants per page. Some merchants' descriptions are very long covering the entire page with lots of enormous graphics. The paragraph description below each company's logo is way too tiny and almost impossible to read; visitors would have to change the font size displayed in their browser window to view the descriptions. It can be assumed that logos are the only thing that the users see while searching for the merchants at Shareasale, so merchants choosing to use the company's platform should make sure their logos are extremely eye grabbing. The banners and text links pages are very bulky and take a while to load. Some of the company's current merchants, especially in the clothing niche are:

Zulilly, The realreal, Inc, Gymboree, Crazy 8 & Janie and Jack, ModCloth, Sheln , Lulus, SA Co, Proozy, CUPSHE, Reebok, gamiss, Soft Surroundings, ChicV, Fashionmia, Inc. SleepyHeads Mall, DressLily, Primary, Trunk Club, Johnston & Murphy, Groopdealz, Sun Frog Shirts, Working Person's Store, Popreal,Inc, Le Tote, Goodnight Macaroon

WebSponsors

Websponsors primarily follow the CPA program. Their time-tracking is almost a day delayed, and the multi-tier marketing is allowed, but you will only get a percentage from your referred site and affiliate. Their application procedure is short, and the major portion is automatic. They send you a link through email to confirm your joining of the network. Like every network that throw the usual caution about the terms and conditions of joining a network, Websponsors go one step ahead and ask for your site's privacy policy. This step ensures the safety of the affiliates and the merchants as well.

Every task in the company's interface is easy to manage. The company provides an option that permits you to add rotating banners to your site that corresponds to profiles you produce. This technique assists you in tracking the ad. While other networks offer the identical feature, WebSponsors interface is just faster and easier to work with.

Another fascinating feature that WebSponsors offers is their co-branding tool. It allows you to build a subdomain of their Free2Try.com and TrialOffers.com. The tool provides an interface, and you can add a logo and header to your subdomain using this interface. You can also select the colors, links, and background for the texts. These kinds of sites can provide you prompt access to your link codes. When you move your cursor over any of the links on either of those sites, your affiliate identity code will be inserted into each of the links.

If you want to promote any one of those offers separately on another site, right-click on the link you want and add it to the new page that you are producing. The only drawback of using those links is that the subdomains are dynamically generated, and the links are changing all the time. If you hard-code a link to another page, you could find out later that the offer has terminated and that you've been sending your subscribers to a broken link. Be vigilant and make sure you don't waste your efforts. Here is the list of some of the company's past clients: TV Guide, The New York Times, Sports Illustrated, People, Time, Money, Fortune, eCompany, Entertainment Weekly, Wall Street Journal, USA Today, MTV, Sony, Seventeen, Rolling Stone, and Forbes Magazine.

Choosing an affiliate network

Choosing an affiliate network can be daunting as there are infinite affiliate networks operational. In this section, some of the

50

questions are provided that should be answered by the affiliate networks. If you can't find an answer on the merchant's site, contact them through mail or phone. If the contact information isn't available on their site, don't waste your time and move onto the next program. If the merchant's response time is delayed (approximately one to two days), I recommend that you move ahead and hunt for other programs. Before contacting the merchants through mail and phone, make sure that you have gone through their entire website, and the answers aren't covered elsewhere. If the answer is already there, it will make a crummy first impression.

As an affiliate who is searching for affiliate networks, you should have the following questions in mind like, which affiliate network is best for your business? What kind of affiliates are most successful in the affiliate network? And which affiliate network will help you to gain more new customers? Finding the answers to these questions isn't as daunting as searching through millions of entries for affiliate networks on Google. For your better understanding and evaluation of an affiliate network, it is advisable to go through a few simple questions that will help you find the best affiliate network for your e-commerce journey.

Following are the questions that should help you determine the best affiliate network for your business.

- **What kind of merchant finds the most value in the particular affiliate network?**

You should ask the affiliate networks to provide you with the list of merchants that are relevant to your niche, and you should be able to find out the reason for their success. This is to confirm the value of your niche in that affiliate network, and you should also get an enormous amount of data of the best categories of merchants working in the affiliate network. It may also give you an idea of intermingling with different merchants that do not suit your niche. For instance, if you deal in electronics, you may want to think about how well your business will perform in a network specializing in medical and health industry.

- **What type of Program they offer?**

As mentioned in the previous chapters, the three essential affiliate programs are: pay per lead, pay per sale, and pay per click. Pay per sale program is also referred to as percentage partners program. These programs pay either fixed amount or a percentage of the sale that is made through your links. Pay per sale program is usually preferred over the other two programs as it is performance based. The other two programs require a large amount of audience to generate some cash. The real essence of working as an affiliate is to add value, and if you target the audience effectively to provide them with what they need, you will be able to earn a handsome reward.

- **Are Sales Statistics Reported in Real Time?**

You can't really wait for a month to find out if you made a sale for a particular program. It isn't possible as you are spending money to promote their product, you can't afford that kind of enormous delay. While signing up for an affiliate program, you should confirm the presence of real-time tracking tool. Real-time tracking tool should not be delayed more than an hour or two. However, the ideal time trackers are prompt and report sales within a minute. CJ affiliates provide the real-time tracking facility. Many competitive affiliate networks provide real-time tracking feature, just make sure the affiliate network you are choosing has it.

- **Is the network safe against scam?**

With the increasing online business, the instances of cybercrime are also enhancing. It has always remained a threat to the performance marketing industry. The scammers usually target the larger brands. However, the small and medium sized business are more vulnerable because of their diminished safety protocols. You should make sure the affiliate network is safe, and also ask for their policy in dealing with scammers in the network.

- **Is the affiliate program multi-tier?**

An interesting way to generate more revenue is through a multi-tier affiliate program. For instance, a two-tier program offers two sources of income, the first by joining the program and the second for referring new affiliates. If affiliate networks allow multi-tier programs, make sure that you go through their terms and conditions. Your fundamental concern is whether the company you are associated with is selling products that provide real value to their customers. Therefore, first, you should focus on marketing the product effectively, and you can think about hiring affiliates of your own later.

- **Is there an Affiliate Agreement?**

Most affiliate programs have agreements that must be signed before entering into the programs. This is to make the process safe for them. However, these agreements are necessary for your safety as well. If your selected program doesn't have an agreement published on their website, simply neglect the merchant and hunt for someone else. Without an agreement, you can easily be swindled.

Creating a substantial ground to evaluate different affiliate networks is probably the most effective way. The information you gathered from the questions mentioned above and other influential factors like upfront cost, contract term, and the payment schedule are all combined to make a decision. The network that resonates with all of your requirements will turn out be ideal for you.

Chapter 5: Compensation Methods for Affiliate Marketing

Predominant compensation methods

Revenue sharing or pay per sale is the most commonly used method of compensation; it is used by around eighty percent of affiliate programs. Cost per action or CPA is used by about nineteen percent. Cost per click or CPC and Cost per mille (CPM) commonly known as the cost per thousand are used by the remainder.

Diminished Compensation Methods

Cost per click or cost per mille are used by less than one percent of the more traditional affiliate programs, at least in the more mature markets. Paid search and display advertising do use these compensation methods a lot, though.

What all that cost per mille require is that the person who is publishing the ad makes it available on his or her website so that page visitors can see it. This is enough to earn commissions. Pay per click goes one step further. It isn't enough that the visitor can see the ad, they must click on it and visit the website of the advertiser.

Cost per click is not used as extensively today as it was when affiliate marketing had just started out. This is because it is quite vulnerable to click frauds that are similar to the click fraud issues faced by modern search engines. When statistics for cost per click are generated, they don't take into account contextual advertising since it isn't very clear whether affiliate marketing includes contextual advertising.

While mature online advertising and e-commerce markets don't use these methods a lot, there are emerging industries where these methods are still in use. A good example of this is China. Affiliate marketing in China can be quite different from what is prevalent in the West. Quite a few affiliates in China are paid by a flat rate or "Cost per day, " and there are networks that offer CPM or Cost per click.

Performance/Affiliate Marketing

When taking into account cost per click or cost per mille, it must be remembered that the publisher will not care whether a visitor is part of the audience that the advertiser wants to attract. The publisher will already have earned the commission simply by putting up the ad or getting the visitor to click on it. Therefore, the entire burden of the risk and any losses if the visitor doesn't purchase anything falls upon the advertiser.

When it comes to cost per sale or cost per action methods of compensation, it isn't enough that the referred visitors merely visit the website of the advertiser. For the affiliate to earn a commission, the visitor must purchase something. Therefore, it becomes imperative that the affiliate identifies targeted traffic to send to the advertiser so that there is more chance that the visitor will be converted. Here the advertiser and affiliate share the burden of the risk and of the loss.

Another name for affiliate marketing is "performance marketing." This refers to the usual method of compensation for the sales employees. Each conversion garners the employees a commission and sometimes there are added incentives if the employees exceed targets. While affiliates aren't direct employees of the advertiser for whom they promote services or product, the compensation models aren't very different from the ones that the advertiser uses with its own sales staff.

"Affiliates are an extended sales force for your business." This phrase is not entirely true. The biggest difference here is that an affiliate marketer will have little to no influence over the visitor's purchasing behavior once the visitor goes to the website of the advertiser. On the other hand, the sales team is there every step of the way right up until the sale is completed.

Multi-tier Programs

There are advertisers that have what are known as multi-tier programs. Under these programs, the commission is distributed into a referral network that is hierarchical in nature. What this basically means is this: marketer A becomes an affiliate and gets a commission for every converted visitor. Now, if marketers B and C also sign up for the program thanks to marketer A and use his or her sign-up code, any future conversions that B and C make will ensure that an additional commission, at a lower rate, of course, goes to marketer A.

Most affiliate marketing programs are only one-tier. There are very few affiliate marketing programs that offer two tiers. Referral programs that involve more than two tiers are similar to network marketing or multi-level marketing but aren't the same. The difference lies in the fact that the commission qualifications or requirements in network marketing or multi-level marketing are more complicated than the ones used by standard affiliate programs.

Chapter 6: Building traffic and cashing the customers

The significance of Web can't be ignored. It has surely surpassed the print media, and almost every business is shifting towards the online zone. The three most important leading advantages of The Web over the traditional printed catalogs are its readiness, inexpensive, and personal nature. The first two advantages are quite obvious as you don't have to wait for the online content to get printed and distributed. It saves an enormous amount of time as your online catalog is instantly available for the customers. Putting a catalog on the Web eliminates the cost of printing, which can result in big savings for you. However, the fact that online catalogs can be more personal is the most important benefit associated with The Web. The personal touch comes from the Web's potential for interactivity. The ability to click links make customers actively involved with your catalog.

The web site is the actual arsenal of an affiliate marketer. Running an online business (especially affiliate marketing) without a website might sound like a joke. This chapter is focused on the different strategies employed while working on your website. It also delves into the different techniques to convert browsers to buyers. Different strategies and ideas to make the site attractive and customer friendly will also be discussed throughout this chapter. So are you ready to take your online marketing business to a next level? Let's go.

Once your website is online, we can move forward to understand the conversion rate. You are probably familiar with the adage that "Build it and they will come." This rule is not just restricted to your website but your entire online experience. Firstly, we will have a look at the concept of conversion rate. Actually, it is the percentage of browsers that become buyers. In simple words, your site's conversion rate is the number of visitors that come to your site and then buy from you. It is concerned with converting the window shopper into a real buyer.

But you should be wondering how to calculate the conversion rate? Well, it is quite straightforward. The conversion rates fall in a wide range depending upon the sites and businesses. Some businesses can go up to about 20 to 25 percent or even beyond while some can be as low as 2 to 3 percent. Let it be a number game, and suppose that 5 percent is a good conversion rate for first-time visitors to your site. So if 500 visitors are daily visiting your site, then at a 5 percent conversion rate your sales should be 25. Keeping this thing in mind, the only way to drive up sales is to enhance traffic.

If you want to run a healthy 5 percent conversion rate, you must be able to figure out the number of visitors you need daily. Follow these steps to get a better idea.

The first and foremost step is to determine the number of sales you need per day to stay in business. It will determine your break- even point. Next, you have to divide the number of sales with your conversion rate (0.05 in your case). This number becomes your targeted goal. Simply, if you want 100 sales per day, your target goal is 2,000 visitors every day.

Some factors might influence your true conversion rate. Keep these factors in mind before getting too comfortable with your targeted goal.

Qualified traffic: If you are shooting in the dark for traffic without the proper strategy, it may unbalance your conversion rate scale. You have to identify your potential buyers by putting efforts into targeting the demographic trend. By doing so, you may attract fewer visitors, but more of them would buy.

Site Design: Everything from the layout and navigation of your home page to your search box and shopping cart affect the prospect that your visitors will be converted to customers. The more engaging, attractive, and advantageous your site, the better your expected conversion rates.

Quality product or service: If you are compromising on the quality of your services, no matter how many visitors you have daily, your conversion rate will be very low.

Price factor: Different pricing strategies can be utilized to uplift the conversion rate unless and until your demand is in conformity with the market price. Otherwise, people will assume that your rates are falsely inflated. However, if you are selling a unique product or well established with your online business, these discrepancies will not influence your conversion rate greatly.

Estimating the time frame when you get the most traffic

You need to have a look at the bigger picture when you are trying to enhance the volume of your traffic to increase your sales. For that purpose, you have to estimate that which part of the day or what time of the day is resulting in bulk traffic to your site. The typical patterns of online traffic can be categorized into four specific segments of the day.

Early morning (6 to 8 a.m.): Most people don't shop during these hours, and different studies indicate that the sales are reduced to almost half in most of the cases during this period.

Daytime (8 a.m. to 5 p.m.): This period is one of the busiest for professionals to spend time online while working. The individuals ranging from 25 to 54 years are the most common buyers during this period. Ideally, the conversion rates for online retailers get a boom between 10 a.m. to 1 p.m. That is because the buyers typically spend their lunch breaks searching the online sites. And surprisingly their search is not just limited to window shopping, they are also willing to make a purchase.

Evening (5 to 11 p.m.): In between the time people arrive home from work and the time they head to bed, they apparently have plenty of time to do a little more online shopping.

Late night (11 p.m. to 6 a.m.): This period also corresponds to diminished sales. However, some night owls are still hunting for deals, but they are in the minority.

Weekend: The conversion rates are almost identical to weekday buying habits, but weekends usually bring a greater number of sales.

The beauty of online business lies in the fact that it is always open, so it never misses a chance to lose a buyer. You can sleep whenever you want while keeping your online business running and who knows you might somehow catch a night owl. Now when you are aware of your traffic habits, you can work your strategies in accordance with the peak traffic times. Here are some critical assumptions that can be drawn from your traffic data.

If your customers are most receptive to the ads, then it is where you want to spend your budget. Your collected traffic data might come handy here as you can decrease spending money during downtimes. Alternatively, the spending amount can be increased during the peak traffic hours. To cut the long chase short, you are now in a better position to allocate your ad budget precisely.

How to enhance the traffic on your site?

You have to be consistent, thorough, and influential in keeping the potential customer stick to your site. Go for the multipronged approach that caters both the online and offline marketing efforts. You can utilize the upcoming techniques to enhance traffic and uplift your conversion rates.

Keyword searches: Paid keywords have proven themselves to be a cost-effective method of attracting targeted traffic to your site.

Natural search: You can hire an SEO expert to rank your site high on the google search. It is a plus if you have adequate knowledge of SEO. It has always remained an important tool to drive the traffic.

External links: If you are looking for qualified visitors, increasing the number of sites that link to your site is usually a good deal.

Similarly, link referrals from online custom reviews and blogs can greatly enhance traffic to your site.

Affiliate traffic: An affiliate program can be set up to help direct traffic your way. But this technique is more favorable once your site is established.

Advertising: The most powerful technique to bring traffic to your site is advertising.

Offline mode: As you are working online, it doesn't necessarily mean that you only have to stick to the online methods of getting traffic. However, promoting your site offline (such as by business cards, word of mouth, and by networking) can help to build traffic, too.

Content: Building attractive content on your site is another way to keep the customer hanging for prolonged durations. As they spend more time, your chances of making a sale are doubled. While creating content, two things should be kept in mind. The first thing is to write unforgettable text. Business writing on the Web differs from other writings that are usually dry in tone. So this is your chance to express the real picture of yourself. In an online environment, sites that are funny, authors who have a personality, and content that's unconventional are most likely to succeed. The second thing is to strike the right tone. You may not know but your business also has a personality, and the more striking its description on your site the better it is. Try to employ the tone that depicts your business uniqueness as it can distinguish you from your competition.

It is not about a specific technique; you can opt any technique that is suitable for your business and is also within your budget. The main thing is to reach the potential buyer with the ultimate goal to relish the long term relationship.

Converting browsers to buyers

Different statistics can be used to measure online business such as the total revenue, total profit, and the total number of customers. However, another important measure to check the credibility of an online business is stickiness. It simply indicates the time a user spends on a particular website. It is the time calculated from the moment an online user visits a website to the moment he/she either moves on to the other website or closes the tab. So it can be assumed that the longer the average time, the stickier the internet business.

The more time that people spend on your website, the greater the chance that they will buy one or more of your products or services. You have to compel people to keep coming back to you. If they are coming back, an increased chance of a sale is what you can get.

Giving Customers a reason to stick to your site

If you are looking for an increased stickiness, there must be a reason for customers to stay on your site, come back, or participate more in your business. Here are some of the methods you can employ to make your online business stickier:

Focus on original content: Regardless of the product, you have to provide original content for your site. The information you provide can be in the form of blogs, articles, reviews, or engaging tips and tricks. Your content must be highly appealing; discussing almost every aspect of the product. It must provide a sense of security to the customers so they can make purchases quickly without fear or hesitation.

Discussion Boards: Discussion boards serve as a mean of bridge between you and your customers. It helps to make an interactive environment, and the product gets more human exposure.

Encourage your customers for reviews: Ask for a favor from your long term customers to contribute towards your site. Their contribution can be in the form of reviews, guides, or even anecdotes. Some businesses also encourage customers to participate in their weekly or monthly contests where the best contributor wins discount vouchers or gifts.

Provide help and support product: Items like FAQ section, support documents, and articles that describe the way of using the product if any must be placed within your site.

Why providing your own content is necessary?

Buyers are always looking for unique and original information that they can't get anywhere else. The reason behind the huge success of Amazon is that it provides tons of customer and editor reviews, how to use guides, and the bestseller lists. Providing information regarding your service or product leads to more sales and happier customers. For instance, if you sell books, write reviews of the new releases for the month. If you sell electronic products, perhaps you can write a guide for shopping the best smartphone and then compare some of the top brands and discuss their characteristics and features. You can always hire a person to write this kind of stuff. However, it is a big plus if you can write these materials by your own.

When you are providing content for the site, don't forget to hyperlink the products you sell. But make sure these hyperlinks and references should not be annoying. Keep it nice and simple, just add a thumbnail picture of the product you are discussing. The customers just have to click that thumbnail to direct them straight to the product page.

Getting other people to deliver your content

Providing the material for your site is not just confined to your contribution. In fact, some of the biggest online businesses rely on others to bring them the content their users depend on. Always think out of the box, and try to encourage the global community to contribute towards your business. You can get the content from:

Suppliers: The manufacturers, suppliers, and distributors you work with are usually trying to build their brands, too, so involving them in your online business is not a bad deal. Let the customers know the latest products coming from your manufacturer.

Media sources: There are tons of organizations that can happily provide you the content for your site without costing a dime. You can try one of these sources like Articles Base, eZine Articles, Go Articles, iSnare, etc.

How can customer logs prove handy?

Customer logs or Web server log file contains information about pages your customers are viewing. As you're working online, you must relish the perks of online business; you can always keep track of the different web pages that customers view on your website. Every time the customer shifts to a new page, a new entry is created in the customer log. You can open your log file and see all your customer activity. The customer log is a text file that your website provider automatically creates and maintains for you.

Going through the customer logs will give you a better understanding of the trends and likings of your customer. After the data is collected, you can delete the content that has become obsolete or customers are no longer visiting it. The basic requirement is to make the shopping experience more streamlined and easy for the customers.

Predicting future purchases

In the internet world with the facility to view the customer logs, you can always make future predictions about sales. Your predictions might prove wrong initially, but with ample experience and exposure, you will be able to master that art too. Comparing the customer logs and their past purchases can prove to be handy. As you have built trust with your customers, they will always come back to you. If the data collected from the customer logs is indicating the increased traffic generated by a particular product, re-stocking that product can turn out be a good option. Of course, you don't require physical space to stock, so the overhead costs will not be the case for you. However, restocking the products that are always in demand is a safe bet, rather than stocking the products that are already low on demand.

For a more accurate estimate to pick future products to stock and anticipate your customers need, look at what they are willing to buy from you today. Some dimensions should be kept in mind as you study the past purchases.

The data containing the average price of an item should be collected. Always consider the affordability of your customers in mind. Keep track of your highest and lowest selling products and their sales comparison data for the better working of your business. After all, if your customers are used to buying latest electronic accessories for less than $300, selling a $1800 laptop might be out of their reach. Furthermore, try to increase your customers' average order amount as it will add value to your business.

The whole concept of the conversion of browsers to buyers can be summarized as follows. According to a study conducted there are two most influential factors for converting browsers to buyers. First, the site's security because buyers tend to make a purchase from the site that is most secure. Second, the multiple options for payments like a credit card, debit cards, and other options like PayPal.

Constructing a buyer friendly site

In the brick and mortar business, being friendly means to greet customer warmly as they enter the store, shaking their hands, and giving them a smile. In a case of an online business, friendly means to create a buyer friendly site that makes sense to buyers

76

and makes their shopping experience comfortable. Keep in mind that they are visiting your business partially and they can always move to the next business by a mere click. Ensure that you provide the basic pieces of information to them, go to your home page to check the answers to these basic questions:

- What is your business?

- What's the principal focus of your business?

- What does your business have to offer to the consumer?

- What makes your business good enough to earn a customer's trust and eventually sale?

- How would a customer start shopping on your site?

If your home page is unable to answer these questions, I am afraid to tell you that your site is not buyer friendly. You need to be straightforward and as direct as possible with your buyers. The buyer with the specific need is at your door; you have to offer the customers a satisfying shopping experience. Let us delve into some further strategies to make the site more attractive and appealing.

Streamlining the shopping process

Building the private area for specific customers as most of the membership sites offer makes the online shopping experience easy. As you are looking for a long-lasting relationship with your customers, retaining their information, so they don't have to re - type the information like credit card number, and all the necessary details again can turn out be a useful facility. This facility saves time, and also most customers find it disturbing to put the details again and again. Their accounts should be already created, so they pop in and get what they want and leave without trouble. That's a great service you can provide on your website, make sure your customers can always:

Reach their shopping carts and accounts: The site should be designed in such a fashion that the customers can always have a look at their shopping carts and account details. Keep it simple, and the best policy in this regard is to place these options on the top of the web page so that they are just a click away.

Special products on the main page: The more accessible your products are, the easier it will be for the buyer to add them to their cart. Don't confuse things and make it as simple as possible.

78

Search box: A search box usually saves time. Your customer just has to put the product he/she is looking for in the search box. Then through automation, your entire inventory can be searched for the product your customer is looking for.

Asking customers for feedback

Feedback is essential for the proper flow of any business. You may find many ideas attractive and even practical also but what if your customer doesn't like them. These kinds of things create a gap between the buyer and the seller. Feedback can fill that void for you. If your customers are giving you a bad response on a certain product, you can immediately work on the flaws of the product to make them sync with the expectation of the customers.

Some strategies for attracting and keeping customers

Let's talk about the ways to attract and keep customers. Obviously, the content of the website is the only way of interacting with the customers in the first place. So the material that you include on your site should be easy for the people to digest (designed in such a way that explains who you are and what you have to offer), be informational and have a friendly tone, concise in length, and clear in its organization.

Developing content for a Web site is knowing what online viewers desire and determining strategies for providing it to them. Identifying your target audience will help you make a personalized message that will make each potential customer think you are communicating directly with him or her. But you should also keep some general concepts in mind that will help you market successfully to all ages regardless of the gender and socioeconomic barriers.

Always remember to keep things clear, and do not provide the content that will be dubious and leaves the customer perplexed. In fact, don't keep anyone in suspense about who you are and what you do. The people who come to a website give that site less than a minute and in most cases even lesser than that to answer their primary questions like, who are you? What's your main theme or mission? What do you have to offer to me? Why should I prefer your site over all the sites that deal in the same product/service? It may sound intimidating and unfair, but most web surfers are thinking that in the back of their mind as they are scrolling through various sites.

When it comes to Web pages, it pays to put the essential components first. As discussed previously these components are who you are, what you do, how you stand out from any competing sites, and contact information. For instance, Profnet's mission statement is just a single phrase. "Helping Business Professionals Find More Business." If you can't find a single phrase to accommodate your entire business, then try to make two to three concise sentences at the most. Ensure that your mission statement is more specific and customer oriented.

If you deal in a lot of products, you probably can't fit everything you have to offer right on the front page of your website. Even if you could, you wouldn't want to as it may look bizarre. For instance, in a television newscast, it's better to prioritize the contents of your site so that the top stories or the best contents appear at the top, and the rest of what's in your line is arranged in order of importance. Furthermore, the content on your site should be organized in such a way that it can be accessed easily.

Offering deals and promotions

Special deals and promotions are the most common way to ask for the sale because you're giving buyers a specific buying proposition. You're offering something to make the deal bigger, whether it's a discount, a free additional item, or an extra service; it entices the customer. Usually, a successful deal or promotion has that critical time limit. You can limit these elements:

The span that an offer is available: "Applicable for the next 12 hours only."

The number of people who can take advantage of the offer: "Only the first 50 customers can get the deal."

The quantity of the product: "Order now - supplies are limited."

A time limit compels customers to act. Otherwise, if an offer is always out there, it's a regular deal and not counted as a special offer.

You can pick from a number of events that can trigger this deal like it could be a customer who registers for the first time or a customer who adds more than ten items to the shopping cart, or the customer who visits your Web site by using a special Web address. It could also be the case when a specified length of time (depends on your choice) has elapsed, and the customer still hasn't added anything to the shopping cart.

Freebie Opportunities

People no matter how well off they may be, usually respond to a good deal. If you are looking to grab the attention of the customers, try using the words like win, free, new, discount, and sale, etc. on your website home page. As you will add these words, you will feel the difference as these offers are usually vital for the boost of a website; will add a good deal towards your business.

Contests and sweepstakes

The word 'free' and the phrase 'Enter Our Contest' can give you an uplift as far as money is concerned when talking in terms of a business Web page. In fact, few things are as likely to get web surfers to click into a site as the promise of getting something for nothing. Giveaways have a number of hidden benefits like anyone who enters the contest, sends his/her personal information that can be utilized to compile a mailing list or prepare marketing statistics. Giveaways get people involved with your site, and they usually come back to you, especially if you conduct contests for several weeks at a time.

Of course, in order to hold a giveaway, you need to have something to give away. If you make baskets or sell t-shirts, you can designate one of your sale items as the prize. If you can't afford to give things like that, offer a deep (perhaps 30 to 35 percent) discount.

You can organize either sweepstakes or a contest. A sweepstake chooses its winner by random selection whereas a contest requires participants to compete in some way. The most effective contests on the Internet are simple and straightforward. If you hold one, consider including a "Rules" Web page. It should elaborate that who is eligible, who selects the winner, and any rules of participation. Furthermore, on the contest rules page, be sure to state the starting and ending dates for receiving entries clearly. Some states have laws regarding the disclosure of this kind of information. Be aware of the federal and state laws and regulations regarding sweepstakes and contests. Such laws often ban illegal lotteries as well as the promotion of alcoholic beverages. Telemarketing is sometimes prohibited in connection with a contest.

84

The techniques and strategies covered in this chapter might be restricted to your website, but they are imperative as your website is your online shop. The conversion techniques are vitally important which can be used to turn browsers into buyers.

Chapter 7: Additional Tips on How to Earn Money as an Affiliate

When you read all the advantages that affiliate marketing has to offer, they might lead you to believe that you can get rich overnight simply by selling affiliate products online. Nothing could be further from the truth. While affiliate marketing might make earning money online sound easy, you need to remember that all those advantages will attract a lot of competition. To make a success of it, you need to know your market, what it requires, how products should be promoted and what is working and what is not. Here are a few tips that can help you cement your success in the world of affiliate marketing.

1. Only Choose a Handful of Good Products

A very common mistake made by a lot of affiliate marketers is registering with a lot of programs and promoting everything. This method will only end up making you feel overwhelmed, and no product will be marketed properly. As I mentioned earlier, it's best to find your niche and promote only a few good products there. Figure out what is needed in the market and sell products that work with the content of your site.

2. Use Several Traffic Sources to Promote Products

Don't just put up ads only on your site. While this approach works, there are so many other sources of traffic that you can use to promote products at the same time as you sell them on your site. Remember, you'll make more commissions if you can send more targeted traffic to the sales site.

One way you can do this is by using Google Adwords. All you have to do is make an ad in your account with AdWords. Next, you need to use your affiliate link in the target page URL of the ad. Of course, common sense dictates that you'll have to constantly keep an eye on the conversions and make sure that the cost of the campaign is less than then profits generated from it so that the campaign can continue to run.

3. Test, Measure, and Track Your Affiliate Campaign

Don't just use one strategy to promote products. Try out a variety of strategies so that you have a good idea of what works and what doesn't. You can try to split test and determine how each campaign is doing and act accordingly. Sometimes, just a few changes can show you a dramatic increase in profit. If you're using banner ads, ensure that they are placed in different areas of your sites pages. Not all positions are equally noticeable.

While a lot of affiliate programs do give you basic information about how you're doing, it is a good idea to use your own conversion software too. You have a plethora of choices when it comes to this software, so pick a good one to track the campaign.

4. Research the Demand of the Product

If the demand for the product that you're selling isn't high, you're not going to sell a lot, regardless of what you do. Before you pick a product, do your research and figure out if that is what your visitors need or want. If you have plenty of people visiting your site, you can ask them directly by conducting a survey.

5. Stay Current with New Methods and Techniques

As I said earlier, the field of affiliate marketing is full of competition and the competition constantly comes up with new strategies and techniques. Ensure that you are au fait with these techniques as well as the latest market trends. You wouldn't want to fall behind.

6. Choose the Right Merchant

Remember, you're not just promoting a product; you're also promoting the company that makes it. Make wise decisions here. You wouldn't want your visitors to be dissatisfied with products you've marketed. You're only shooting yourself in the foot if you don't pay attention to that. If you want to maintain long-term credibility, look for companies and websites that offer good customer service.

7. Use Helpful Tools

If this isn't just a side earning for you, if you're determined to make this your business you need to use tools that help you work efficiently. Fortunately for you, there are plenty of such tools available. For example, if your site is powered by WordPress, you can get a plugin like the Affiliate Link Manager.

Chapter 8: Managing affiliate business

Managing the affiliate business data is one heck of a task if you are working manually without the help of affiliate marketing tracking software. Whether you have one site with two or three affiliate programs or five sites with multiple affiliate programs, you need to keep track of your affiliate data. Keeping track of programs joined through an affiliate network is stress-free, as you will have only one username and password to remember. Once you've logged into the interface, you can access statistics and get banners and ad copy for all the merchants associated with that network. On the contrary, most of the stand-alone programs you join will have different login information. If you've got a good memory, perhaps you can memorize all that data, but the rest of us usually need assistance to keep track of all that information. Let's have a look at some of the tracking software.

Cake

Cake is a complete management tool when it comes to tracking and optimizing the affiliate networks. If you are looking to view the overall performance of your networks, review and analyze results, and manage contacts under one hood; cake can make that happen for you. However, these are not the only characteristics catered by this software, some of the additional characteristics are: Various payout layouts, concurrent metrics, targeted campaigns that can be customized by location and devices, scam prevention facilities, separate portals for clients or affiliates, pixel and post back management, and round the clock availability of help desk.

The software is categorized into three discrete tiers- Select, Pro, and Enterprise. However, the price is usually based on the usage.

HasOffers

Hasoffers – An affiliate marketing tracking software created by twin brothers Lucas and Lee Brown was an instant success when it hit the market in 2009. This white-labeled software was innovative, reliable, easily accessible, and flexible. Some of the exciting features include a two-way API, infinite number of affiliates, scam protection facility, a mailing room, committed solutions option, and the facility to transform currencies. It has something extra to offer, besides tracking your affiliate networks, you can also advertise your online business through this distinctive software. You can try the free trial of the software for a month. If it fascinates you, select either the Pro ($279/month), Enterprise ($799/month) for further usage.

LinkTrust

Another tracking software, although a bit old, but still doing well. LinkTrust launched their software in 2002. They claim to be the most accurate software in the market. The software comes with a customizable interface that can be adjusted according to your preferences. It allows you to track any kind of advertising activity whether online or offline. You can view and manage the cookies, pixels, server posts, CPA, CPC, pay per call, and even mobile traffic. They also provide the best support in the shape of patented LinkTrust RTA (Remote Traffic Agent). LinkTrust has a three-tier system as far as pricing is concerned: Advertiser (Initial setup $600, $575 monthly), Network (Initial setup $2000, $1750 monthly), and Lead Gen (Initial setup $500, $1250 monthly).

OmniStar

Another veteran in the field of affiliate marketing tracking software is OmniStar. They have been working for thirteen years and claim to be the leading tracking software in the market. The software is easy to use and install. In fact, the initial setup only takes 10 to 15 minutes. It is integrated with multiple payment formats, OSI affiliate software, and helps you to connect with new customers through social media and upgraded SEO facility. The company offers five pricing packages ranging from $47.95 to $297.75 monthly. You can easily select the package that suits your business need.

Impact radius

It was founded in 2008 by experts who previously launched savings.com. Some of the appealing features provided by Impact radius are: Mechanization of contracting, onboarding, tracking, reporting, and payment of direct affiliates, absolutely accurate tracking facility, flexible tracking approaches through Pixel, file transfer protocol (FTP) file upload, and data post, tracing of promo codes, call tracking, SEO friendly links, real-time metrics, and ad hosting as well. The pricing details can be fetched from the sales department.

iDevAffiliate

iDevAffiliate also claims to be the number one affiliate tracking software product. Even if there is some exaggeration, the fact can't be denied that this popular software is competing in the market since 1999. The incredible features include; customization of the payment structure, promoting offers and deals through banners, creating reports that compile the daily activity data and track marketing stats. Furthermore, the software is also equipped with a built-in shopping integration feature that is linkable to most carts and checkout systems. The company categorizes the software into four pricing options viz. the Standard edition for $149, the Gold version for $249, the Platinum version for $349, and the Black version for $399.99. However, if you don't want to buy the software, you can lease it for a monthly fee.

Lead Dyno

Once you have provided the sign-up information, Lead Dyno spontaneously creates an affiliate sign up page for you so you can begin your proceedings of receiving traffic from affiliates. You are also provided with a customizable page that track visitors, leads, and clients. You can even track your Adwords campaign. Lead Dyno comes with an enthralling feature that helps to invite people to join your network of affiliates. The staffing program is easy to handle, and the invitation is sent via

94

an email. Lead Dyno offers three pricing options that are pretty much affordable. They charge on a monthly basis with the starter package at $49, the accelerator at $79, and the rainmaker$149.

AffiliateWP

AffiliateWP is favorable for people who are using WordPress for their website or blog. If you are one of them, then you should take advantage of this software. This plugin promotes your products and services. However, the task is not just restricted to promotion, it also helps to integrate the most popular e-commerce plugins for WordPress and offers actual time reporting and management of your affiliates. The software accurately tracks affiliate referrals through caching and has one of the best support systems in the tracking software industry. In the most latest and advanced versions, more extensive add-ons like lifetime commissions and recurrent referrals are offered. The company provides three pricing options. These are Personal at $49, Business at $99, and Developer at $199.

Hit Path

Hit Path is one of the quickest and most comprehensible affiliate tracking software present in the market. The software has an impeccable multichannel tracking platform that can be customized according to your personal preference and need. Some of the enticing features include; free training program, round the clock availability of support desk, real-time campaign tracking, affiliate management and incredible reporting scheme, accounting module, and a white-labeled interface. The free sign up trial is also available.

Click Inc

If you are not familiar with HTML, try Click inc as it provides the simplest of interfaces to deal with. Click inc further streamlines things by upgrading the SEO through Trulink format. This format will help link directly to your sales page instead of highlighting it in a coded link. Other exciting characteristics include; reports on traffic status, notifications and graphs containing click dynamics, commission, and sales. Moreover, some other management tools help you to create coupons, tier based commissions, and to communicate with merchants. The starter plan can be taken for $25 a month. However, the advanced versions are priced at $69 and $149 per month.

Now you are familiar with some of the affiliate tracking software; I leave the choice of selecting the software on you. With the assistance of the software, you will be able to perform your affiliate managing tasks at a much higher speed and efficiency. Dividing the tasks into discrete sections is vital for the better working of the business. The tasks can be divided as:

Regular Tasks

To keep your business on track, there are various undertakings that should be performed on day by day, week after week, month to month or quarterly premise. Utilize the accompanying recommendations as a rule for making your own particular support plan.

Daily Tasks

As an affiliate marketer, you won't get that much **E-mail** related to your business. Merchants don't communicate that much via e-mails unless there are some new offers to disclose. However, they usually send out the occasional affiliate newsletter. Same goes for the affiliate networks, which will only notify you of the new merchants and those who are leaving the network. As far as customers are concerned, you won't get many emails from customers, as the vast majority of those will be coordinated to the dealer. Be that as it may, on the off chance that you do get email questions about items or administrations offered on your site, react expeditiously with either the reply or an offer to divert their question as suitable. Both the customer and the merchant will perceive and value your exertion. Since the customers made the inquiry, it implies that they are fascinated with your site, and are most likely wanting to purchase the item.

Another important consideration to check on a daily basis is: **Webpage Monitoring** - Is your website on the web? On a Daily premise place your URL into your browser's address bar, refresh the page and discover!

The peril in not realizing that your site is down when you are running a compensation for each click promoting the effort. Obviously, the pay per click cost includes whether your site is working or not. In the event that your site is down, you are paying for promoting, yet nobody is purchasing. Just in case the idea alarms you, NetMechanic is a service that will verify whether your site in on the web, like every fifteen minutes, 24 hours a day. In the event that your site is down, they'll tell you by numeric pager, alphanumeric pager, or email, so you can

98

resolve your downtime issues quickly. Look at their free trial, which will check your site every fifteen minutes for 8 hours, so you can perceive how their administration functions.

Link Checks - Broken links are the most despicable aspect of any affiliate advertiser's presence. It's simple enough to ensure your links are working by routinely utilizing one of the accompanying services like Netmechanic.com, and siteowner.com

Check Statistics- Checking your statistics daily for each network and individual affiliate partner is necessary, especially when you are new to the affiliate business. Sort your daily revenue data with the aid of an accounting software.

Weekly Tasks

Include and Submit New Pages - Add another page of substance to your site each week to keep it new. This will urge your guests to continue returning. Make certain to present your new pages to the real web crawlers.

Include and Submit Keywords - Always be watchful for new watchwords and catchphrases to add to your pay per click advertising campaign. Scribble down your thoughts and after that add them to your Overture, Findwhat and different platforms on a week after week premise.

Examine - Spend some time each week surveying and inquiring about the news in your industry as well as Internet showcasing news. Finding out about new techniques and instruments for working together can spare you time and cash not far off.

Monthly Tasks

Distribute Newsletter - Stay in contact with your site's guests by dropping them a note or pamphlet at any rate once per month. Share news and give them yet another motivation to come back to your site.

End of Month Statistics - Tally your wage and costs once every month to remain on top of your general business picture. Enter information into your spreadsheets to see the direction of your traffic and sales conversion.

Quarterly Tasks

Launching a New Site - Diversification is an ideal approach to fence your wagers against critical showcase changes. With the advancement in technology and the increasing demands of the customer, you should always be looking for some substantial

100

changes that follow the on-going trends. If you opt more of a static approach, you will fall flat, not far off. So, be prepared for positive change.

Chapter 9: Ways to promote the affiliate business

Unfortunately, the adage, "Build it, and they will come" doesn't fit the web. Instead, growth on the web is a hard-fought conquest. You have to actively market your site to get the word out for attracting visitors. In this chapter, we will discuss different techniques to promote the affiliate business. First, we will learn some quick methods to get traffic, and then we will shift towards some of the free ways to get traffic.

Ways to get traffic fast- Quick Promotion Techniques

If you are looking for a quick response, it goes without saying that you have to spend some money. Let's have a look at some commercial ways to get the traffic real quick on your site.

Google Adwords

Google with over 3.5 billion searches every day is surely the most leading search engine if we talk about surfers, especially online shoppers. That is why advertising with Google Adwords is considered the quickest way for the online market exposure. The ads start running within a few minutes after your payments are cleared. Google offers two exciting advertising facilities viz. the Google Adwords and the Google's Premium Sponsorships (detailed account will be discussed later).

Ads that are displayed in small rectangular boxes usually on the right side of the Google search page are from Google Adwords. However, your ads may be displayed on Google directory, Google groups, and Google partner sites as well. Google AdWords have attracted millions of advertisers for its simplicity and prompt response. It is the most reliable targeted cost per click (CPC) advertising, regardless of the amount of your budget. Creating a Google Adwords ad is a straightforward task, you are just required to write a description, choose keywords that are most relevant to the listings and finally determine the amount you are willing to pay per click. You actually pay when someone clicks on your ad. However, if you are running low on budget, the Adwords Discounter is another fascinating tool that helps to reduce your cost per click payment so that your ad keeps running on the result pages. There is no activation fee, and you only have to pay for the actual clicks. The data of your ad performance can be retrieved online from the control center.

Your ad's positioning depends on how often your ad is opened through surfer based clicks, so it can be said that the better the ad, the higher it will appear on the page. On the contrary, if an ad has an overall 0.5 percent click-through rate (considered as an underperformance), Google sends advice in the form of an email suggesting the wise choice of relevant words to enhance the performance of an ad. The essential part of the Google Adwords campaign system is its flexibility. The tools like geo-targeting help you to address the surfers appropriately regardless of their location. Furthermore, at the campaign level, you are provided with the facility to choose your daily budget and can also set a time frame for the advertising of a specific product. For each campaign, there is an Ad Group level at which you create ads and choose keywords. However, you can also create multiple ads in the Ad Group that will rotate evenly when surfers search on those keywords. In conclusion, if you are looking for a cost per click advertising, Google Adwords must be added to your arsenal.

Pay per click search engines

The second quickest way to gain internet exposure is to purchase keyword listings on pay per click search engines. You may wonder how the pay per click advertising work. Actually, advertisers bid on relevant keywords and pay the amount bid each time someone clicks on the link that leads to their site.

It is always surprising when a newbie Internet marketer is waiting for their site to get listed by the free search engines and hasn't yet opened up a pay per click account. This approach worked several years ago, but now it is obsolete. You can now wait months or even years for your site to get uplifted by the free search engines, and end up 678th or 3,658th in the search listings. Even showing up 50th, won't bring you enough traffic in a week to get yourself a new pair of shoes. That is why it is wise to invest in pay per click search engines. I recommend you to start with the accounts on Overture, Findwhat, and Kanoodle. Besides these, some of the engines that will bring you the highest amount of targeted audience at reasonable prices are 7search, Serach123, ah-ha, Searchfeed, Turbo10, and Xuppa. Once you start getting plentiful traffic to your site, you can opt the search engine that suits your demand.

Yahoo Listing

You can pay Yahoo! for the listing of your site. According to Alexa rankings, Yahoo is at number fifth (in terms of traffic generation) both globally and in the US as well. It gets an enormous amount of traffic, and that's the biggest reason behind listing in Yahoo's human-compiled directory. It is a quick way that leads Google to pick up your homepage, and a link from Yahoo will also enhance your Google page ranking. Yahoo's link is not obligatory, Google can still find your page, but if you are looking for a lot of traffic quickly, Yahoo's listing is where you get it.

Google Premium Sponsorships

Google's another intriguing tool is their premium sponsorships, although expensive but remarkably helpful. If your advertising budget is high, Google premium sponsorships allow you to purchase exceedingly targeted advertising on the most pertinent search engine on the Web. Whenever your purchased keywords and phrases are searched by an online surfer, no more than two enhanced text links appear at the top of the Google search results page. The compensation method employed by Google Premium Sponsorships is CPM or cost per thousand impressions. You can estimate the feasibility by comparing the average conversion rate and the price of your product.

E-Zine Advertising

Numerous E-Zine (online magazines) publish daily on the internet. Placing your ad in e-zines is a cost effective way to bring qualified traffic to your site. You just have to find the e-zine that suits your niche. The directory of E-zines is an exceptionally helpful resource that will help you find e-zines that can bring traffic to your site. The following sites will help you to place your ads in the most relevant e-zines. For instance, bestezines.com, Directoryofezine.com, e-zinez.com, lifestylespub.com, etc.

Build an Opt-In Subscriber List

Permission marketing is an approach to sell products/services to specific people who have already shown consent to the delivery of the marketing information. Opt-In email is the best example of permission marketing, and this technique actually works in the affiliate marketing environment. In fact, building an opt-in list is the most cost effective and precious method of marketing on the Internet. As your subscriber has willingly signed up or opted to receive the information, it allows you to: Offer new products and services to the client, get information about a certain product through surveys based on the opinion of the subscribers, and most importantly you build a long lasting relationship with the subscriber. Studies have revealed that permission emails are ten folds better than the banners when talking in terms of response rates.

Once you have built a list of a few hundred subscribers, keeping that list up-to-date on an ongoing basis can be an intricate and time-consuming process. So, it is recommended that you use a professional "mailing list service" to keep on top of your lists for you. These services automatically handle all your sign ups, unsubscriptions, and bounces. The biggest advantage of having a professional service which maintains your mailing list is that it protects you from spam complaints. Most affiliate networks that permit email marketing of their merchants' offerings insist that you be able to produce evidence of subscriber opt-in. Having a mailing list service will also prevent your ISP from closing your account down because you consumed up too much of their bandwidth by sending 30,000 emails to your subscribers. To set up your opt-in mailing list, I highly recommend that you try out one of the following autoresponders and mailing list services like aweber.com, getresponse.com, etc. They are inexpensive and will save your tons of manual labor. Many affiliate marketers miss a trick of creating a mailing list, and they eventually end up on the losing side. I am sure you don't want to be on the losing side, so try to build your own mailing list.

Publish a newsletter, eCourse, or both

Marketing is all about attracting visitors, and many internet marketers encourage visitors to join their mailing list by offering a free newsletter. If published properly and regularly, an excellent newsletter can bring visitors back to your site over and over again; it gives the visitor a reflection of what you have to offer. The newsletters can be utilized to inform subscribers about the special promotions and deals offered by the merchants. If you want to keep track of the new visitors, try to direct the visitor to the sales page located on your site before he/she actually goes to the merchant's site. That way you will have a better knowledge of the efficiency of your newsletter.

The best way to go about it is to have your mailing lists set up to deliver a pre-determined number of messages after someone subscribes to your lists. The pre-programmed messages are a series of autoresponder messages that get sent to subscribers at specific intervals. For instance, a 'Singles eScene' opt-in list delivers a series of pre-programmed messages related to

Internet dating. The first message should be delivered immediately after sign-up, and then another message in the series should be sent to the subscriber every ten days for the following 5 weeks. But what happens after the 5 weeks are completed?

You can broadcast messages to your list of subscribers at times and intervals of your preference. So, if a merchant comes up with a great offer that your subscribers should love to hear about, you just need to blast a message to them at any time.

If you have a long list of subscribers to that particular mailing list, the effect would be fairly immediate and always positive. People would rush off to the site to take advantage of the offer, and you would just get a nice little bonus for doing this simple task (Although, building a mailing list is a tough ask). Yes, you must build an opt-in subscriber list. Then you have to do something with it. Publish a newsletter, develop an e-course or do both. If you are not building a mailing list or allowing it to waste away in the computer storage, you are actually losing money. You may wonder how? Let's have a quick look at some number game. Say you have 1,000 unique visitors who come to your Web site in an average week. Even though they had an

110

initial interest in your site's material and subject, the vast majority of these people will never be back, just because they will forget you after some time, or won't remember how to access your site. Now imagine, if you had a free newsletter or course to offer them in exchange for their opt-in information like name and email address. At a sign-up rate of 10%, you'd be getting 100 new opt-in subscribers per week or 4,800 per year. These are people who are giving you the authorization to send emails to them over and over again in the future. I hope you don't miss out on this dominant marketing opportunity.

Use Auctions to sell affiliate products

eBay gets an enormous amount of traffic daily, and they have hosted over 5 billion auctions so far. That's a huge market, and one of the leading reason for affiliate marketers to opt for a way to promote their products. Keep in mind that some affiliate products can't be sold directly on eBay's site. Ensure that you have gone through the rules and regulations before rushing off to start listing your affiliate products. Despite the restrictions, there are ways to use eBay's phenomenal market reach to promote your affiliate business. For instance, suppose you sell electronic products as an affiliate. Clearly, you know a great deal about the products you sell, so utilizing that knowledge about electronics you can write a report like '4 charismatic android devices to buy'. Within the report, you dexterously incorporate affiliate links to your merchant's site. Make sure that the report is downloadable, and if you are able to sell some copies; you can cover some of the insertion and eBay store subscription charges. However, your ultimate success lies in the fact that with each report sold, buyer's email address is added to the arsenal of your mailing lists. Not to forget, the affiliate product links incorporated within the report are the source of increased revenue as they are generating traffic on the merchant's site. Be prepared for some report writing because you can use auctions to sell your affiliate products for real. Apart from eBay some of other online auctions are bidz.com, uBid.com, and Yahoo, etc.

Ways to promote affiliate business for free

Now you are familiar with the commercial methods to promote the affiliate business, let's explore some ways to promote your affiliate business without spending a dime.

Joint ventures

The joint venture is a mutually beneficial program. Suppose you deal in health and fitness products, your first aim should be to find a person who is associated with the health and business field. Once you have picked up the right person propose him/her to accompany you to market your affiliate product. Once they agree to lend you a helping hand, you can ask them to promote your affiliate business on their homepage. Every time a buyer buys one of your products through their links, you can favor them with split revenues. That's the mutual benefit of a joint venture.

In reality, joint venture partners (affiliates) sell far more products than you can do on your own; which is the second benefit. Joint venture partners will serve as your sounding board. They will be the ones to reach out to other likeminded health conscious people who are interested in the health and fitness products and then they, in turn, will become affiliates essentially growing your company. It gives rise to a chain reaction, and this is what an Internet marketer is looking for.

The whole process has a lovely synergistic effect. On the other side of the coin, you may start getting many joint venture requests each and every day.

Write E-zine articles

If you are running low on budget, and want to save some of the advertising expenses; writing e-zine articles is one of the most effective and least costly ways to entice visitors to your site.

Over 3.5 billion people are using the Internet every day to find information. To fulfill this exceptionally growing demand, e-zine owners who don't have time to write their own material are always hunting for new articles to publish in their newsletters.

Writing a short "how-to" or "tips" article on a topic relevant to your Web site theme is no different than writing a letter, or conversing with a friend. Simply share authentic and exciting information that determines your enthusiasm for the subject and inspires the reader to learn more. The most compelling reason to write articles for e-zines is the amount of money you save in advertising. A single e-zine ad can cost anywhere from a few dollars to thousands of dollars.

However, e-zine article submissions are free. In fact, some publishers actually pay you to write and submit articles to e-zines and newsletters.

114

You can add your acknowledgment at the end of each article, along with your short personal biography and your site's hyperlinked URL. Publishers who use your article are bound to publish all of your information as submitted. Now, that's an influential free advertising way to benefit from. Furthermore, the author's resource box, in which your byline is placed, is usually the size of a typical e-zine advertisement. So, you have managed to save advertising dollars and in the long run you earned ten times more of the coverage than before. That is a great return for the time you put into writing the articles. Depending on the subscriber base of the e-zine that selects your article for publishing, the potential for new visitors to your site could be massive.

The written articles should be added to your site, and you should also find means to spread these articles on different forums and websites. Onsite archiving has a supplementary benefit. As more of your articles and links to your site appear on more and more pages, the popularity of you link will increase a great deal. With the increased exposure and link popularity, your name becomes widely renowned, and your credibility as an expert in your field enhances. This effect becomes amassed, as specialists are often interviewed for other publications which again upsurges their popularity bar.

Besides popularity, the friendliness that you build by teaching and sharing your experiences generously with your readers is the real success. You also perpetually get more knowledge about the topic you write about which further empowers you to write more in future. Utilizing this upbeat approach for the promotion of your site builds traffic faster, and is much less time-consuming than the search engines that can promote your site. When your articles are published in e-zines relevant to your site's topic, people who are interested in your niche read them. With your accomplished and explanatory tactic, interested readers become interested visitors, who in turn become driven purchasers, and then repeat buyers. This methodology is not bad at all; you are just investing an hour or two on writing and most importantly you don't have to spend any money. Some of the e-zine article submission sites that will help you to get started are ideamarketers.com, marketing-seek.com, and makingprofit.com, etc.

Free Directory listings

Yahoo (as discussed earlier is not free) contains a large internet directory, but in this section, we are focusing on the free methods of promotion. Your site can be submitted to open directory project (dmoz.org) which is the largest human edited directory present on the web. There are numerous categories and subcategories within their database, and you will definitely find your niche as well.

Search engine and crawler listings

The crawler is a program that systematically surfs the World Wide Web to create entries for the search engine index; that means your site automatically listed without the submission. Of course, if you want to be picked up by the crawlers, you need to have solid links that direct to your site. Yahoo listings guarantee the Google's crawler visit to your site. Getting recognition from different search engines is a huge plus, and the secret lies in your page optimization.

Groups and forums- A platform to connect to buyers

Different groups and forums can be used as the source to find potential buyers. Google, Yahoo, MSN, and other major platforms have discussion groups in which you can participate and post messages. However, it is better to research the groups before posting. Avoid blatant advertising, instead respond to another group members with helpful information. It is the best way to gain respect and credibility in the groups. The prime goal of participating in groups is to connect to potential buyers. You need to arouse interest in people, so they want to learn more about you. Make sure that you are providing them links to your site.

Trading and Promotion

You may wonder how trade and promotion are linked. In fact, they are linked through link exchanges. Link trading is also known as link exchange, or reciprocal linking is an online promotion strategy employed by affiliate marketers and site owners to amplify link popularity to bring a large number of targeted traffic to their sites.

Page ranking in search engines is highly dependent on the link popularity of your site. Link popularity is determined by the collection of sites that link to yours, as well as the reputation of those sites. The search engine rankings are highly controlled with these kinds of factors. You've probably seen sites with separate sections dedicated to links. These sites have listed links that they have traded with their companions. Links that are placed on your page from another site should include your site's name or principal keywords. This will ensure the optimal popularity of your website.

Link popularity is enhanced when popular sites (SEO ranking wise) are associated with your site. If you are looking to add real value, look for links that are somewhat identical to your niche; the most relevant the best. The popularity of you link can be destroyed if you exchange links with websites that are in the same category as your own. Link trading carries major drawback that is the reason why it is important to select those sites which have a large targeted audience. As you have placed links on your site, you are actually redirecting your customers to your competitor's site; they leave your site without buying, in most cases.

The same principle is followed by banner exchanges and FFA (Free for all) programs. They also have the identical drawbacks.

So, before putting other's link on your site, make sure that it gives your affiliate business an overall advantage.

So,

Start page networks

If every hit counts, then you might want to consider start page networks to entice free traffic to your site. Here's a quick guide on how these products work. Simply, sign-up and enter some basic information about the page that you want to promote. Set the Traffic Swarm code as your home page. Earn credits when you open your browser. Earn more credits when your friends sign up and open their browsers. The more credits you have, the instances your site will show up on other members' browsers increase. Your links are then displayed all over the network to comparable website surfers. Traffic Swarm automatically includes your site in the TrafficSwarm Search Engine. Specifically, your links are displayed when other network users open their web browser. Get started with an account on trafficswarm.com

Chapter 10: Mistakes Affiliate Marketers Make

Since affiliate marketing programs are easy to become part of and pay commission on a more or less regular basis, many people join up. However, if you want to succeed in this field, you need to be consistent, and you need to have a marketing strategy that is effective. Therefore, it is absolutely essential that you use the best techniques available and try to avoid making mistakes.

Here are thirteen common mistakes that affiliate marketers make. Don't forget; these mistakes can be quite harmful to the growth of your business. It becomes essential for affiliate marketers to avoid making these mistakes and also find solutions wherever possible.

1. **Not Concentrating on the Pre-offer**

   Excessively numerous affiliate marketers focus on offering the administrations and results of a customer or telling potential clients the negative and positive parts of specific items or administrations. At the point when an affiliate marketer invests a ton of energy attempting to portray items/administrations of a customer or noting all questions in regards to the customer, he/she makes an enormous fumble. The significant objective of an affiliate marketer ought to be pre-offering the customer. As an affiliate marketer, you ought not to offer uncertain data to planned clients.

2. Promoting Products and Services Without Using Them

A few web marketers and website admins make a noteworthy screw up by advancing administrations and items they don't utilize. At in the first place, it might appear to be okay. In any case, after further examination, you will find this is a gigantic oversight which can cost your affiliate marketing endeavors. At the point when a client purchases an item from a sales representative who has been utilizing a similar item, the client has more prominent trust in the item. Similarly, an affiliate marketer can't be effective in publicizing or advancing an item they have not attempted or utilized some time recently. For instance, you can't advance PC recreations in the event that you don't play them.

As an affiliate marketer, you ought to maintain a strategic distance from this misstep by obtaining and investing energy to comprehend the item. Regardless of what the item is, you ought to utilize it to have a hands-on-approach. Potential customers will believe you more since they will see that you are a bona fide individual who is advancing an item from a state of learning or encounter and not a point of voracity. As opposed to committing this error, take as much time as is needed and turn into a client of the administration or item.

3. **Lacking an Email List**

An email rundown is a crucial segment of affiliate marketing. By keeping up an email show, you get the chance to publicize a customer's administrations/items to potential clients over and over. By the by, on the off chance that you do not have an email show, you lose the opportunity to contact a colossal gathering of people, in this manner minimizing the possibilities of up-offer. You ought to maintain a strategic distance from this mess by guaranteeing that you have an email list.

4. **Picking the Wrong Affiliate Program and Product**

124

Not all affiliate projects might be the best for you. Most affiliate marketers pick programs that compensate high commissions or those that offer items/benefits the marketers have utilized some time recently. These components don't really imply that you have picked the right program. An affiliate marketer ought to consider payout, convenience and time while picking an affiliate program or item to advance. To abstain from committing this error, you ought to consider how much time you have to devote to an item or program to wind up effective. Select projects that you can serenely advance inside a specific time span without overstretching yourself. This will go far in helping you to end up a fruitful affiliate marketer. In affiliate programs, payout or commission is an imperative viewpoint. While selecting an affiliate program, guarantee that you adjust commission per deal with the measure of exertion/work or time you will require devoting to pre-offer an item. Ordinarily, these two segments go as one. Additionally, guarantee that the affiliate program you join is genuinely usable and will offer an incredible support of potential clients. At the point when a program is really usable and gainful to customers, a marketer gets to be energetic and enthusiastic about that item or administration.

5. Not Dedicating Yourself to the Marketing Program

There are various affiliate programs. Subsequent to selecting the right program, guarantee that you devote and confer yourself to the program. Affiliate marketing requires a great deal of tolerance, exertion and responsibility for one to be effective. It additionally requires plentiful time to construct and keep up a client base. To abstain from making this screw-up, calendar your time legitimately. Designate abundant time for the program notwithstanding when you are making great deals or the business is developing. Your dedication will pay off at last when clients return over and over to see what new administrations or items your program are advancing.

6. Promoting an excessive number of Services or Products

As an affiliate marketer, you can't be effective by advancing excessively numerous affiliate administrations or items in the meantime. In many occasions, affiliate marketers select such a large number of items in the conviction that they will acquire a tremendous rate of commission or payout after these items are sold. Be that as it may, potential clients are just inspired by valuable items. You ought not to advance a few items at the same time since you won't have the capacity to calendar enough time for every item. This implies a drop in deals. The answer for this screw up is to concentrate on expanding deals instead of expanding the quantity of affiliate administrations and items.

7. Promoting Poor or Low-Quality Products

Advancing low-quality items is another element that can be considered as an affiliate marketing botch. Quality is the vital inclination for every single customer. On the off chance that you are an affiliate marketer and you are advancing low-quality items, your site guests will simply avoid those items. Also, if, by luckiness, they happen to buy such items, never again will they purchase items through your site.

Along these lines, it is indispensable that you make a relationship of trust amongst you and your clients and advance important items. A fulfilled client won't just come back to your site additionally prescribe your site to his/her

127

associates and companions. So by advancing profitable items, you are hitting two winged creatures with a similar stone. You increment your client list and additionally hold your present clients. Along these lines, it is essential to ensure that the affiliate item you are advancing is something that is genuinely usable and significant to individuals.

8. Not Having a Blog or Website

When you are an affiliate marketer, you will not become successful by only promoting affiliate services or products through things such as mailing lists, social media sites, or paid advertisements.

A blog or website is a useful medium to promote your affiliate services or products. Your blog/website serves as a showcase that promotes the affiliate products under your professional name. Your website or blog will help you to establish your niche and originality in front of potential clients. It reinforces confidence in the minds of your website visitors.

A blog or website serves a useful medium that turns your website visitors into loyal customers. In addition, it proves to be a time saving and cost effective technique to market affiliate services or products. So it is very important that you have a website or blog if you want to be a successful affiliate marketer.

9. No Keyword Research

Keyword research is a very important factor in affiliate marketing. You are likely to lose a lot of traffic if you do not use the proper keyword research. Actually, by undertaking thorough and comprehensive keyword research, you get to know precisely what people are looking for when searching for the services or products. Keyword research, therefore, helps you to develop your web page, or home page appropriately, do well with SEO, and to utilize those target keywords that can bring a large amount of traffic to your site or blog. Therefore, keyword research is very important for successful affiliate marketing.

10. Not Writing Quality Reviews

Quality reviews from previous customers can help promote the affiliate products while also providing information about the affiliate products or services. People want to have some knowledge about the services or products that they want to purchase. They like to know the benefits, pricing, and features. A quality review gives them the basic and desired information that they desire to know in an easily laid out manner, so it becomes easy for them to understand what the product is all about. You can confuse potential buyers when you do not provide quality reviews. When there is little to no clarity all about a product, the prospective buyer may decide not to purchase from you, and go elsewhere. In short, to become successful as an affiliate marketer, it's highly important that you provide quality reviews about the products that you promote.

11. Depending on Just One Source of Traffic

If you really want to be successful as an affiliate marketer, you should never rely on only one source of traffic. You should take every effort to maximize your varying sources of traffic so that you can receive visitors from several sources. The sources of traffic can be a variety of areas; social media sites, search engines, and even advertisements. It is important to utilize several channels that can bring a lot of traffic to your website and thus can promote and expand your affiliate marketing.

12. Not Believing in Yourself

If you are not confident that you are going to succeed as an affiliate marketer, then more than likely you won't. It is perfectly normal to be concerned as you begin a new venture and attempt to direct all of the new information related to affiliate marketing. However, it is important to have confidence in yourself as well as your ability in order to become successful in this business.

While success is not wholly based on the belief that you can be successful, it is a highly important for individuals that are earning cash through affiliate marketing. Be sure to take the time to understand the errors and know the programs to avoid; only then, you can have faith in yourself and your ability to enjoy making money with your affiliate marketing business.

13. Believing That Get Quick Money

Affiliate marketing is not a way of getting rich quick, but a way of making money. If you are under the impression that affiliate marketing will make you large amounts of cash in a quick timeframe, then you will quit when you fail to reach your goal.

Affiliate marketing takes consistent attention on your part to turn it into a successful business model. You need to understand that business, which gives quick cash, is not a stable business and can never be a permanent source of income.

Chapter 11: Advantages of Affiliate Marketing

Affiliate marketing, as described by the experts, is a combination of 4 elements containing the brand, customer, affiliate(s) and the various offers for the affiliates that they can choose from to promote the product. It is known to be the cheapest marketing strategy to earn the highest monetary rewards. Just like its counterparts, this strategy has its own set of advantages as well as disadvantages for the ambitious marketers out there. This chapter discusses 8 major advantages of this marketing style that the affiliate marketers of the modern business world should be careful about.

The advantages obtained by the affiliate marketers are as follows:

1. Can Sell the Product Directly
The biggest advantage to the affiliate marketers is that it is not required to produce the product or create its value but rather start selling it right away to the target audience. They can simply choose from the ocean of products or services and start putting their efforts in generating leads or sales to

134

benefit the brand as well as ensure monetary gain for themselves. The affiliate marketers are required to obtain the affiliate marketing links and push/sell the product instantly. There is no worry regarding how the products will be shipped or how much it costs and other such mundane details.

2. Just One Area to Focus on

The affiliate marketer can concentrate only on the affiliate hyperlinks that he has generated or gathered over time and does not need to involve himself in the core business stages such as manufacturing or shipping the product to the stores or the buyers' doorsteps. He is not at all concerned with the money transactions that happen when a product is sold, and the sale is closed. The only thing he needs to put his efforts into is the promotion of the product and to bring in higher and higher numbers of leads for the brand it is affiliated with. Only advertising, the affiliate hyperlinks of the product(s) or service(s) creatively, and earning the rewards are the crux of the job done by the affiliate marketers.

3. No Huge Monetary Investment Involved

This may sound good for the up and coming affiliate marketers who are wanting to step into the intricate and complex world of affiliate marketing. The free tools out there can prove to be very helpful in the beginning when you have less money to invest and are not completely aware of the nitty gritty of this marketing style.

4. Explore Different Marketing Worlds

To begin your work as an affiliate marketer, you should first choose a market that is highly relevant to the products or services you wish to sell. If you notice that there are marketers who are earning a good amount of money by selling a beauty product, then you should invest some time in understanding his affiliate marketing strategy and finding some more related products. After this, launch an SEO or PPC campaign or post some interesting and engaging content of the same to make the readers aware of it and to attract them to generate leads.

5. Earn, Earn and Earn More!

Once you have smartly executed the affiliate marketing strategy, you are in for a surprise! Any of the traditional marketing techniques such as SEO, PPC or content marketing can be used to promote the product as a part of affiliate marketing. Once the hyperlinks are appropriately placed online, you just need to watch out for an email that shows the amount of money you have earned from the sales generated from your efforts online. It is the creativity of an affiliate marketer that helps him earn the rewards sooner or later. There is no need to run here and there, and everything can be done with the help of a computer and an internet connection as well as a desire to be creative and increase your bank balance.

The advantages enjoyed by the brand are as follows:

1. More Leads in Less Time

Affiliate marketing is becoming important in the present day world of fierce competition because of the simple reason that it has a catalytic effect on the overall sales process of the brand. When the company is promoting its products through the affiliate marketers and their website, in addition to its ongoing promotion campaign launched on its own

137

website, the whole marketing effort gets a wheel that rotates only to generate more and more leads that have strong potential to close the sales and bring in the revenue. The focused efforts in just one direction of a product or service promotion act as a boost for the web traffic towards the main website of the brand. So more money is earned in much less time.

2. Delegating Is Earning

The affiliate marketers are taking care of the most difficult part of the sales cycle, i.e. the product promotion in order to beat the competition. When the affiliate marketers are taking care of the product promotion, then there is no need to look out for other ways to promote your unique product, but there comes a necessity to make it even more unique and affordable. As discussed in the previous point, you need to invest your energies in choosing the right affiliate and then channel your efforts into upgrading the product and watching the business growing at an amazing pace.

3. More Market Share with the Same Efforts

In order to succeed through affiliate marketing, a brand needs to select an affiliate marketer who can give him maximum benefits as opposed to any random one. An affiliate marketer who has a website designed for himself and is engaged in a business related to the brand is the aptest choice for a business association. The visitors at his website will see the ad of your product or service and will surely visit your website to know more about the product if everything goes well in between, and the experience he gets from the website of the affiliate business is good enough to continue with. Hence, it is an easy way to grab a larger market share.

Chapter 12: Disadvantages of Affiliate Marketing

While it is easy to go overboard upon seeing the advantages of affiliate marketing, the above chapters show you that it is easy to make mistakes in this business. As such, you also need to know about the dark underbelly that this business has before you decide to venture into it.

Here Are the Biggest Disadvantages of Growing Your Affiliate Marketing Business

1. Affiliates Come and Go

When you first start out as an advertiser with an affiliate program, you'll find that the curious visit you in droves. There may even be plenty of excitement – at first. It isn't long, though, before the next e-commerce sensation bursts upon the scene, and your affiliates move away from you.

Another thing to keep in mind is that affiliates keep a very close eye on their commission reports. They even check these reports more than once in just one day. If they see that earnings have decreased for even a small amount of time, they can get quite jittery.

140

2. Affiliate and Network Commissions Will Fade Your Bottom-line

If you consider the best case scenario, affiliates help you boost your sales.

However, this increase in sales comes with some additional costs. The commissions you pay out to your affiliates are generally in the range of five to ten percent. On top of that, if you've joined affiliate networks, you have to pay them too.

3. Profits May Decline by Routing Through Affiliates

This one is a major disadvantage but something that a lot of e-commerce sites don't always take into account. Consider the following scenario.

So you've started out, and the number of sales is very encouraging indeed. You haven't yet started using affiliates. When you finally do sign some up, the number of sales goes up. That's great, isn't it? However, you'll come back down to earth with a bump when you realize that your aggregate sales level hasn't changed much. Why? Well, that's because your affiliates convinced a visitor to come to your site using a link with an affiliate code. The direct sale becomes something that makes you pay out commissions to the affiliates.

Now you'll want to know how this happened. Well, there are plenty of methods available to them such as SEM, SEO, fake promotions, creating fake coupon codes and so on. An affiliate could even pull off something like ensuring that the only way a visitor comes to your site is by clicking on their link.

4. Affiliates May Not Treat Your Brand with the Respect and Care it Deserves

You spend a lot of time, money, energy and creativity in coming up with the concept of your brand and developing it. Then you get an affiliate who doesn't care about your brand at all. The next thing you know, you're having to deal with issues created by affiliates messing up the image of your brand or even completely misrepresenting what you offer.

Other Disadvantages and Issues with Affiliate Marketing
Past and Current Issues

Ever since affiliate marketing came on the scene, there haven't been effective controls in place with regards to how affiliates operate. Everything from false advertising to spam to adware to forced clicks has been utilized by the unscrupulous affiliate so that their links drive traffic to the advertisers. While affiliate programs do have rules against spamming as part of their terms of service, affiliate marketing has been vulnerable to spammers.

E-mail Spam

When affiliate marketing was still in its nascent stages, there was a lot of negative press thanks to affiliates who used spam as a means of promotion of their programs. However, now more and more affiliate merchants have included terms and conditions that state clearly that affiliates are not allowed to spam.

Search Engine Spam

As search engines have come into their own, spamdexing has become a major issue. This is where an affiliate creates web pages that are automatically generated. These web pages generally have merchant provided product data feed. The whole point of these web pages is to manipulate how prominent or relevant resources indexed by a search engine are.

Earlier, websites that only contained affiliate links had a low reputation because it was believed that they did not deliver quality content. Google made changes in 2005 and classified certain websites as "thin affiliates." These were either relocated to a lower position or removed entirely from the search results. Now affiliate marketers must have content that is good in quality on their websites, or they will fall under this category.

Consumer Countermeasures

To be effective on the internet, affiliate marketing relies a lot on different techniques that have been built into a web page and website designs. It also relies on calls made to external domains so that user actions can be tracked and advertising can be made available to the user. First of all, all of this takes time. Secondly, casual users of the internet consider this a nuisance or visual clutter. As such, many countermeasures have been developed to stop advertising from showing up or to remove it when web pages are rendered. There are many third-party programs such as Adblock Plus, Ad-Aware, Spybot and other pop-up blockers that remove the visual clutter efficaciously and save time and bandwidth that would normally go when the web page is rendered. A system's exposure to malware can also be reduced by entering precise information in the HOSTS file. This blocks persistent and notorious click tracking and marketing domains.

Adware

While adware is not the same thing as spyware, it does utilize the same technologies and methods. Earlier merchants did not have much information about adware, its impact and how it negatively impacted their brands. Affiliate marketers were the first to pick up on the problem. This was because they realized that tracking cookies are overwritten by adware, and as a result, commissions reduce. Those affiliates who did not use adware considered this a theft of commission. In fact, adware is not useful to the user and often the user has no idea that adware has been installed on their computer.

Internet forums became discussion hotspots for affiliates to discuss the problem of adware and how to tackle it. Affiliates became more organized and started asking merchants not to use adware to advertise. They exposed merchants who didn't pay attention to their demands or who actively supported the use of adware and tarnished their reputations as well as their efforts to sell through affiliate marketing. In fact, a lot of affiliates simply stopped selling for such merchants. Sometimes, they even moved to competing merchants. Ultimately, affiliates and merchants put a lot of pressure on affiliate networks to prohibit specific adware networks. A Code of Conduct was created by Linkshare's Anti-Predatory Addendum, beFree and Performics/Commission Junction and ShareA Sale, who banned the use of software applications to promote advertisers' offers. However, no matter how many regulations have been put into place, adware is still a problem.

Trademark Bidding

When the first pay per click engines came out in the late 1990s, some of the earliest adopters of pay per click advertising were affiliates. Google Adwords was launched in 2000. It is a pay per click service by Google and the reason that pay per click is widely accepted and used in advertising today. When more and more merchants tried to use pay per click advertising, whether it was through a search marketing agency or directly, they found their affiliates already in that space. While this state of affairs was responsible for a lot of debate and strife between affiliates and merchants, the biggest problem was that affiliates had started bidding on the names, trademarks and brands of the advertiser. Therefore, a lot of advertisers included terms in their affiliate programs that did not allow affiliates to bid on such keywords. There are always exceptions, however, and the advertisers still exist who not only tolerate affiliates bidding on their trademarks but actively encourage it.

Compensation Disclosure

The FTC has created disclosure guidelines that publishers such as bloggers may not know about. These guidelines directly impact the language used in advertising, endorsements by celebrities and compensation presented to bloggers.

Lack of Industry Standards
Certification and Training

At the moment there are no industry standards for training and certification in the field of affiliate marketing. Certain courses and seminars do offer certifications, but these certifications are accepted mostly because the company or individual who offers or issues the certification has a good reputation. This field is not a common field of study at universities or business schools. There are very few college instructors who, in conjunction with internet marketers, try to educate marketing students about this subject.

Most often people learn about this field only in real life by joining up and learning 'on the job' as it were. While many books on this subject have been published, not all of them are reliable. There are those that encourage readers to adopt unscrupulous practices such as manipulating holes in the Google algorithm. They may even suggest techniques that affiliate programs and advertisers specifically prohibit.

When it comes to program management companies that are outsourced, they generally give a combination of informal and formal training which consists of brainstorming and group collaboration. These companies also ensure that their marketing employees get to go the industry conferences that they prefer.

Podcasts, online forums, specialty websites, weblogs and video seminars are some of the other tools that can be used for training.

Code of Conduct

In December 2002, affiliate networks beFree and Performics/Commission Junction released a Code of Conduct that is meant to ensure ethical practices and standards in online advertising.

Sales Tax Vulnerability

The State of New York asserted tax jurisdiction over Amazon.com sales that had been made to the residents of New

York in April 2008. They did this by inserting an item into the state budget and based it on the fact that websites based in New York had affiliate links to Amazon. The state said that Amazon has a business presence in the state as long as there is even one such link and that this is enough to let the State of New York tax all the sales that Amazon made to residents of the state. Amazon did take legal recourse but lost in January 2009 at the trial level. Right now the case is being heard by the New York appeals court.

Cookie Stuffing

Cookie stuffing is a method meant to create income for the person who is doing the cookie stuffing. In this method, an affiliate tracking cookie is placed on the computer of a visitor to the website without their knowledge or consent. First of all, this method creates affiliate sales that are fraudulent. In addition, it overwrites other affiliates' cookies, thus stealing commissions that they have earned legitimately.

Conclusion

Now we come to the end of the book. I hope that with what I have written you have gained a good perspective on what affiliate marketing is, how you can break into the business and what you need to watch out for.

We have discussed affiliate marketing and its components in detail. We have also looked at how it came to be and how you can break into this field. We have looked at strategies you need to employ to become a successful affiliate marketer and things you need to avoid. We have also discussed the affiliate networks in detail. The ways to promote and manage the affiliate business are also quite elaborative. We have also talked about the advantages and disadvantages of this field. Bear in mind, it's never too late to practice an idea, don't be afraid of the consequences, and the fear of failure should not hold you from trying something new.

I do hope that you enjoyed reading this book. Feel free to leave a review about how this book helped you. Thank you for your purchase!

Free Bonus: Join Our Book Club and Receive Free Gifts Instantly

Click Below For Your Bonus:
https://success321.leadpages.co/freebodymindsoul/

64794188R00087

Made in the USA
Lexington, KY
20 June 2017